# Media
# Ownership

# Media Ownership

The economics and politics of convergence and concentration in the UK and European media

## Gillian Doyle

SAGE Publications
London • Thousand Oaks • New Delhi

First published 2002

 SAGE Publications Ltd
6 Bonhill Street
London EC2A 4PU

SAGE Publications Inc
2455 Teller Road
Thousand Oaks, California 91320

SAGE Publications India Pvt Ltd
32, M-Block Market
Greater Kailash – I
New Delhi 110 048

**British Library Cataloguing in Publication Data**

A catalogue record for this book is
available from the British Library

ISBN 0 7619 6680 3
ISBN 07619 6681 1 (pbk)

**Library of Congress Control Number available**

Typeset by Keystroke, Jacaranda Lodge, Wolverhampton
Printed and bound in Great Britain by Athenaeum Press, Gateshead

# Contents

# Acknowledgements

I would like to express thanks to those who agreed to be interviewed for this study and, in some cases, who provided access to company accounts and research reports. I am grateful for the generosity and candour of interviewees (who, for reasons of confidentiality, are not individually named) at EMAP, Granada, Grampian Television, Guardian Media Group, Mirror Group Newspapers, News International, Pearson, Scottish Media Group and United News & Media. I am also very grateful to interviewees at the Department of National Heritage (now the Department of Culture, Media and Sport) and at DG15 of the European Commission. Some of the work presented here has, in earlier versions, been published. Chapters 2 and 9 draw on a report carried out on behalf of the Council of Europe (MM-CM) in 1998 (Doyle, 1998a). The research findings discussed in Chapters 4 and 5 were reported in more detail in the *Journal of Cultural Economics* (Doyle, 2000). Some aspects of the findings set out in Chapters 7 and 10 were discussed in previous publications by the author (Doyle, 1997, 1998b, 1998c, 1999). My thanks to Philip Schlesinger of the Stirling Media Research Institute for guidance and encouragement. Thanks also to Julia Hall at Sage for helpful advice.

# 1

# Introduction

The so-called digital revolution is transforming media and communications industries worldwide. Media companies in the US, Europe and elsewhere are keen to take part in the changes and, if possible, to emerge at the forefront of an increasingly transnational and competitive communications marketplace. The volume and scale of mergers and alliances involving media players that has taken place in recent years has raised considerable challenges for regulators and state authorities across the globe. This book examines how media policy-makers in the UK and Europe have responded and it assesses the main socio-political and economic implications of recent shifts in media and cross-media ownership policy.

In some respects, technological advances appear to have encouraged greater diversity throughout the media. Entry barriers have been coming down in many sectors and not only has the number of broadcast channels in Europe multiplied rapidly since the early 1990s but the recent growth of the Internet has also introduced a diverse array of new players. But, at the same time, digitization and converging technologies have encouraged strategies of expansion, diversification and ever-increasing concentration of ownership amongst leading players in the media and communications industries. This new era of consolidation of ownership and mega-mergers presents European regulators and policy-makers with complex and difficult challenges.

The prevalent impetus towards deregulation of conventional broadcasting and press ownership restraints is usually explained in terms of a need to allow domestic players to exploit important new economic and technological opportunities, preferably ahead of international rivals. Drawing on empirical research carried out in the UK, this book sets out to explain exactly what sort of economic benefits result from greater concentrations of media ownership. It investigates the commercial and strategic advantages of consolidation and cross-media expansion and the extent to which press and broadcasting interests are actually converging. The socio-political and cultural consequences of permitting concentrations of ownership in the media sector are extremely profound and these are also examined and explained.

Ownership of the media is a 'hot' political topic. In many European countries, policies to deal with media concentrations have been reviewed in recent years and, in some cases, radically revised. This book analyses how policy-makers in the UK and at the European Commission have weighed up and responded to competing concerns surrounding the development of large media conglomerates. In so doing, it seeks to open up for question the capacity of existing mechanisms for policing the media to cope with influential corporate media interests.

## Why are media firms expanding?

An important reason why media firms are expanding is because the traditional boundaries surrounding media markets are being eroded. National markets are being opened up by what is sometimes referred to as 'globalization'. 'The communications revolution has . . . caused an internationalization of competition in almost all industries. National markets are no longer protected for local producers by high costs of transportation and communication or by the ignorance of foreign firms . . . Global competition is fierce competition, and firms need to be fast on the uptake . . . if they are to survive' (Lipsey and Chrystal, 1995: 258).

The emergence of a borderless economy and more international competition has naturally affected media markets and firms across the globe (Alexander et al., 1998: 223). The transnational integration of what were previously thought of as just national markets through, for example, the European Union and North American Free Trade Agreement (NAFTA), has accelerated the process. Throughout the 1990s, policy-makers in the US and Europe sought to develop initiatives that supported the development of a 'Global Information Society'. To some extent at least, their hopes have been realized by the dramatic growth of a truly trans-national and borderless distribution infrastructure for media in recent years – the Internet.

So, changes in technology are also helping to diminish traditional market boundaries. And it is not just geographic market boundaries that are being affected but also product markets. Technological convergence has blurred the divisions between different sorts of media and communication products and markets. The term 'convergence' is used in different ways but, generally speaking, it refers to the coming together of the technologies of media, telecommunications and computing. It is also used sometimes to denote greater technological overlap between broadcasting and other conventional media forms. Digital technology – i.e. the reduction of pieces of information to the form of digits in a binary code consisting of zeros and ones – is the driving force behind convergence. Sectors of industry that were previously seen as separate are now converging or beginning to overlap because of the shift towards using common digital technologies.

The implications of convergence are far-reaching. With the arrival of common digital storage, manipulation, packaging and delivery techniques for information (including all types of media content), media output can more readily be repackaged for dissemination in alternative formats. For example, images and text gathered for a magazine, once reduced to digits, can very easily be retrieved, reassembled and delivered as another product (say, an electronic newsletter). So, digitization and convergence are weakening some of the market boundaries that used to separate different media products.

Convergence is also drawing together the broadcasting, computing and IT sectors. According to some, '[u]ltimately, there will be no differences between broadcasting and telecommunications' (Styles et al., 1996: 8). More and more homes are now linked into advanced high capacity communication networks and, through these, are able to receive a range of multimedia, interactive and other 'new' media and communication services as well as conventional television and telephony. Because of the potential for economies of scale and scope, the greater the number of products and services that can be delivered to consumers via the same communications infrastructure, the better the economics of each service.

The ongoing globalization of media markets and convergence in technology between media and other industries (especially telecommunications and broadcasting) have caused many media firms to adapt their business and corporate strategies accordingly. As traditional market boundaries and barriers have begun to blur and fade away, the increase in competition amongst the media has been characterized by a steady increase in the number of perceived distributive outlets or 'windows' that are available to media firms.

The logic of exploiting economies of scale creates an incentive to expand product sales into secondary external or overseas markets. As market structures have been freed up and have become more competitive and international in outlook, the opportunities to exploit economies of scale and economies of scope have increased. Globalization and convergence have created additional possibilities and incentives to re-package or to 'repurpose' media content into as many different formats as is technically and commercially feasible (e.g. book, magazine serializations, television programmes and formats, video, etc.) and to sell that product through as many distribution channels or 'windows' in as many geographic markets and to as many paying consumers as possible.

The media industry's response to these developments has been marked. Media firms have been joining forces at a faster pace than ever before. They have been involved in takeovers, mergers and other strategic deals and alliances, not only with rivals in the same business sector, but also with firms involved in other areas that are now seen as complementary.

Convergence and globalization have increased trends towards concentrated media and cross-media ownership, with the growth of integrated conglomerates (e.g. Time Warner/AOL, Pearson, Bertelsmann etc.) whose activities span several areas of the industry. This makes sense. Highly concentrated firms who can spread production costs across wider product and geographic markets will, of course, benefit from natural economies of scale and scope in the media (DTI/DCMS, 2000: 50). Enlarged, diversified and vertically integrated groups seem well suited to exploit the technological and other market changes sweeping across the media and communications industries.

At least three major strategies of corporate growth can be identified and distinguished: horizontal, vertical and diagonal expansion. A 'horizontal' merger occurs when two firms at the same stage in the supply chain or who are engaged in the same activity combine forces. Horizontal expansion is a common strategy in many sectors and it allows firms to expand their market share and, usually, to rationalize resources and gain economies of scale. Companies that do business in the same area can benefit from joining forces in a number of ways including, for example, by applying common managerial techniques or through greater opportunities for specialization of labour as the firm gets larger. In the media industry, the prevalence of economies of scale makes horizontal expansion a very attractive strategy.

Vertical growth involves expanding either 'forward' into succeeding stages or 'backward' into preceding stages in the supply chain. Vertically integrated media firms may have activities that span from creation of media output (which brings ownership of copyright) through to distribution or retail of that output in various guises. Vertical expansion generally results in reduced transaction costs for the enlarged firm. Another benefit, which may be of great significance for media players, is that vertical integration gives firms some control over their operating environment and it can help them to avoid losing market access in important 'upstream' or 'downstream' phases.

Diagonal or 'lateral' expansion occurs when firms diversify into new business areas. For example, a merger between a telecommunications operator and a television company might generate efficiency gains as both sorts of service – audiovisual and telephony – are distributed jointly across the same communications infrastructure. Newspaper publishers may expand diagonally into television broadcasting or radio companies may diversify into magazine publishing. A myriad of possibilities exists for diagonal expansion across media and related industries. One useful benefit of this strategy is that it helps to spread risk. Large diversified media firms are, to some extent at least, cushioned against any damaging movements that may affect any single one of the sectors they are involved in. More importantly perhaps, the widespread availability of economies of scale and scope means that many media firms stand to benefit from strategies of diagonal expansion.

In addition, many media firms have become transnationals – i.e. corporations with a presence in many countries and (in some cases) an increasingly decentralized management structure. Globalization has encouraged media operators to look beyond the local or home market as a way of expanding their consumer base horizontally and of extending their economies of scale. For example, UK media conglomerate EMAP acquired several magazine publishing operations in France in the mid-1990s and has since expanded heavily into the US market. French media company Vivendi, a majority shareholder of Canal Plus, has pay-television operations in several national markets across Europe and recently acquired Universal film studios through its takeover of Canadian company Seagram. Swedish group Bonnier which specializes in business news and information recently expanded into the UK with the launch of a new daily newspaper called *Business AM* in Scotland.

The basic rationale behind all such strategies of enlargement is usually to try and use common resources more fully. Diversified and large scale media organizations are clearly in the best position to exploit common resources across different product and geographic markets. So, enlarged enterprises are better able to reap the economies of scale and scope which are naturally present in the industry and which, thanks to globalization and convergence, have become even more pronounced.

This points towards what Demers calls the 'paradox of capitalism' – that intensified global competition results in *less* competition over the long run (Demers, 1999: 48). Even with a loosening up of national markets and fewer technological barriers to protect media incumbents from new competitors, the trend that exists in the media – of increased concentration of ownership and power into the hands of a few very large transnational corporations – clearly reflects the overwhelming advantages that accrue to large scale firms.

## Why study media concentrations?

The issue of who owns the media, and how much of it they own, matters. As explained in Part I, it is important for broadly two reasons. The first is pluralism. A great many writers have focused attention on the potential harms that may result from concentrated media ownership, including the abuse of political power by media owners or the under-representation of some significant viewpoints.[1] Individuals and societies have a need for diverse and pluralistic media provision. Concentrations of media ownership narrow the range of voices that predominate in the media and consequently pose a threat to the interests of society.

Recognition of the need to safeguard pluralism has historically been the main reason for regulating ownership of the media. However, concentrated media ownership matters to society, not only because of pluralism and democracy, but also because ownership patterns may affect the way in which the media industry is able to manage the resources available for media provision. Restrictions on ownership could, for example, result in A duplication of resources which prevents the industry from capitalizing on all potential economies of scale. The ways in which ownership patterns affect the economic strength and efficiency of the sector are not solely a matter for broad societal interest but are obviously of immense and particular concern to media firms.

Industrial or 'economic' arguments favouring a more liberal approach towards concentrations of ownership seem to have become more influential in determining media ownership policies in the UK and Europe since the early 1990s. The elevation of industrial interests may, at least in part, be attributed to 'technological mystique' surrounding developments such as convergence and globalization and to the perception that policy-making ought to help industry capitalize on such developments (Hitchens, 1995: 640). But relatively little work has been done to quantify precisely what efficiency gains or other economic benefits or, indeed, what disadvantages greater concentrations of media ownership might bring about. This book sets out to uncover, based on the experiences of leading UK media corporations, exactly what sort of economic or commercial advantages are created as media firms enlarge and diversify.

Above all, ownership and control over the media raise special concerns that do not apply in the case of other sectors of industry. Media concentrations matter because, as exemplified in the notorious case of the Berlusconi media empire in Italy (and, on a lesser scale, as frequently evidenced elsewhere), media have the power to make or break political careers. As was said of a former UK media baron: 'Without his newspaper, he is just an ordinary millionaire. With it, he can knock on the door of 10 Downing Street any day he pleases' (Financial Times, 2000: 24). Control over a substantial share of the more popular avenues for dissemination of media content can, as politicians are well aware, confer very considerable influence on public opinion.

So policies that affect media concentrations have very significant political and cultural as well as economic implications. As these policies undergo sweeping 'reforms' to cater for the perceived needs of an increasingly dynamic media and communications environment in the 21st century, it is important to question whether the structures we are left with adequately safeguard the need of European citizens for media plurality. This text traces the development of media ownership policies in the UK and at the European level since the early 1990s. Taking account of the conflicting objectives that policy-makers have been faced with, it analyses key shifts in position and assesses who stands to gain or lose out from the wholesale redesign of media and cross-media ownership policies.

## Layout of the book

This book is divided into four parts each organized around a specific theme. Part I asks, 'Why does ownership of the media matter?' It examines how society is affected by media concentrations and it outlines the main public interest goals for media ownership policy. It explains, first, the socio-political and cultural concerns associated with media empire-building and, second, the broad economic or industrial policy priorities surrounding media ownership.

Part II investigates, in closer detail, the relationship between media ownership restrictions and the economic performance of the media. This section is based on original research focused on a number of leading UK media firms including EMAP, Granada, News International and Pearson and it examines how exactly media firms benefit from strategies of horizontal, diagonal and vertical expansion. Part II investigates the extent to which press and broadcasting interests are actually converging and, more generally, it unravels the economic implications of policies that encourage monomedia expansion and cross-media diversification.

Part III, again based on original research, focuses specifically on UK media ownership regulation. It analyses how the media ownership rule changes in the 1996 Broadcasting Act came about. It also examines the changes in policy proposed in the 2000 White Paper on communications. The UK case provides a revealing account of the pressures and difficulties faced by national policy-makers in seeking to negotiate the conflicting public interest policy priorities surrounding media ownership. It demonstrates the crucial significance, in the reshaping of rules on media ownership, of underlying power relations between politicians and media owners.

Part IV examines relevant developments across Europe. It traces recent trends in media ownership within other European member states such as Germany, France, Italy and the Scandinavian countries and it explains the different approaches and policy instruments used to promote pluralism and regulate media concentrations. Part IV also considers the likelihood of a shift in responsibility for media ownership regulation to the transnational European level. It explains the political controversies and legal and practical obstacles that continue to deter progress towards a collective European Union (EU) policy approach to media ownership. It reviews the role played by EU competition law in promoting media diversity and pluralism and addresses the question of whether regulation of media ownership can now be left to competition-based interventions alone.

# 1

# Why Does Ownership of the Media Matter?

# 2

# Media Concentrations and Pluralism

The sorts of public policies which are, or ought to be, adopted in order to deal with concentrated media ownership depend on what impact such concentrations are thought to have on the collective good of society. This is a complex and, at times, controversial issue. Notwithstanding the concerns and anxieties raised as large commercial firms accumulate increasing control over the media, the benefits associated with fostering strong indigenous media players have tended to receive considerable airplay in national debates about media ownership policy.

Both this chapter and the next are devoted to examining why concentrations of media ownership matter. They investigate how society is affected by media concentrations and summarize the main public interest goals associated with media ownership policy.

The tendency towards expansion and conglomeration by media firms generally raises two different sorts of policy concern. The first category, which is dealt with throughout this chapter, relates to the potential socio-political and cultural implications of media empire-building. Such concerns focus on the threat to 'pluralism' posed by concentrated media ownership. A second set of issues relates more specifically to the economic implications of allowing media concentrations to develop. The economic policy concerns associated with media ownership are introduced in the next chapter and investigated in further depth throughout Part II.

## What is pluralism?

Pluralism is generally associated with diversity in the media; the presence of a number of different and independent voices, and of differing political opinions and representations of culture within the media. Citizens expect and need a diversity and plurality of media content and media sources.

The need for diversity and pluralism is sometimes associated with the more fundamental right to freedom of expression, as set out in Article 10 of the European Convention (Lange and Van Loon, 1991: 13–26). Without an open and pluralistic system of media provision, the right to receive and impart information might well be curtailed for some individuals or groups within society. The Council of Europe, which is responsible for ensuring compliance with the Convention, has long taken an interest in the issue of how media concentrations affect pluralism. Its Committee of Experts on Media Concentrations and Pluralism (MM-CM) has defined pluralism in the following terms:

> media pluralism should be understood as diversity of media supply, reflected, for example, in the existence of a plurality of independent and autonomous media and a diversity of media contents available to the public.

According to MM-CM's definition, pluralism is about diversity within what is made available, rather than within what is actually consumed. It is about public access to a range of voices and a range of content, irrespective of patterns of demand. The definition of pluralism embraces both diversity of *ownership* (i.e. the existence of a variety of separate and autonomous media suppliers) and diversity of *output* (i.e. varied media content). It is useful to distinguish between these two concepts. A related distinction is drawn sometimes between the idea of 'external' and 'internal' pluralism. External pluralism exists when there is a range of suppliers (diverse ownership) whereas internal pluralism (i.e. pluralism within the firm) is about diversity of content. The latter might be achieved through codes or regulations encouraging diversely sourced, unbiased output. According to MM-CM's definition, the existence of pluralism requires both a diversity of media owners and a diversity of media output.

More generally, the concept of pluralism is comprised of two aspects. 'Political' pluralism is about the need, in the interests of democracy, for a range of political opinions and viewpoints to be represented in the media. Democracy would be threatened if any single voice, with the power to propagate a single political viewpoint, were to become too dominant. 'Cultural' pluralism is about the need for a variety of cultures, reflecting the diversity within society, to find expression in the media. Cultural diversity and social cohesion may be threatened unless the cultures and values of all groupings within society (for example, those sharing a particular language, race or creed) are reflected in the media.

## Concentrated media ownership and pluralism

Despite much hand-wringing about the relentless rise of 'moguls' such as Berlusconi and Murdoch, surprisingly little empirical research has been carried out to pinpoint the impact on socio-political and cultural pluralism of more concentrated media ownership. The main perceived danger is that excessive concentration of media ownership can lead to over-representation of certain political viewpoints or values or certain forms of cultural output (i.e. those favoured by dominant media owners, whether on commercial or ideological grounds) at the expense of others. But in practice, it is no easy task to isolate the role played by ownership patterns in determining what range of media output is made available to the public.

Concentrations of media ownership may involve a number of alternative configurations. 'Monomedia concentrations' (horizontal) refers to concentrated ownership within a single sector of activity, e.g. newspaper publishing, radio or television broadcasting. Cross-media concentrations – sometimes referred to as 'multimedia' concentrations – reflect either vertical or diagonal integration, or both. 'Vertical integration' refers to common ownership across different phases in the supply chain for a media product, e.g. television programme-making (production) and television broadcasting (distribution). 'Diagonal integration' means common ownership between different media sectors e.g. television and newspapers, or newspapers and radio.

In whatever form they take, media concentrations imply that the supply of media is dominated by few rather than many different owners. As a matter of logic, it might be inferred that there is a negative correlation between levels of market domination and levels of pluralism – i.e. that higher levels of concentrated ownership represent a reduction in the number of different independent suppliers and, in turn, the range of output in any given market. Higher levels of market domination means fewer competing suppliers; fewer competing suppliers implies less pluralism.

However, the relationship between concentrations of media ownership and pluralism is not quite as straightforward as this. As discussed above, the concept of pluralism embraces both diversity of *output* (content) and diversity of *ownership*. To the extent that large organizations may be better placed than small ones to innovate in products and to add to the range of media output, an apparently contradictory case may be argued: namely, that concentrated ownership actually increases pluralism. Higher levels of market domination means fewer competing suppliers; fewer competing suppliers implies a more cost-effective use of resources; the availability of more resources for innovation implies an increased range of output; more diverse output implies greater pluralism.

Pluralism is not simply about the presence in a given market of several different products, or even several separate suppliers, for their own sake. The need for pluralism is, ultimately, about sustaining representation within a given society for different political viewpoints and forms of cultural expression. Any specific market (as defined by product and location) can support only a certain level of supply. The composition of that supply raises concern, not only in terms of how many separate products or suppliers are present but, as a related issue, how many products or suppliers will include representation of indigenous political and cultural matters. Thus, in smaller markets, the relationship between concentrations and pluralism will be complicated by the economic question of what level (and composition) of diversity is affordable.

In short, the relationship between pluralism and media concentrations is complex, and both may be affected by a number of issues. It helps to understand this relationship when 'media concentrations' are situated within a broader framework of interrelated forces which may have some impact on pluralism. Mortensen and Sepstrup (Mortensen, 1993) have proposed the following equation, where pluralism is seen as a function of several other variables $(X_1, X_2,$ etc.), including the size of the market and resources available within that market, structural aspects of the media system, and the objectives and competitiveness of media companies (cited in MM-CM, 1997: 56):

$$\text{Media pluralism} = f\,(X_1, X_2, \ldots X_n)$$

## Determinants of media pluralism

The existence of media concentrations constitutes only one variable within a broader framework of issues which might have some sort of impact – either positive or negative – on pluralism. Consequently, the public policy measures which might serve to promote pluralism are not confined to those which affect ownership of media. For example, pluralism may be enhanced by providing extra resources or public subsidies so as to extend the diversity of media output in a given market (Lange and Van Loon, 1991: 44–53). Nonetheless, media concentrations are obviously a key variable within the equation.

What is of central interest here is the nature of the relationship between concentrations of media ownership and pluralism. Figure 2.1 sets out some of the main factors which are likely to have a bearing on levels of pluralism. Diversity of media ownership (or 'diversity of suppliers') is clearly a highly

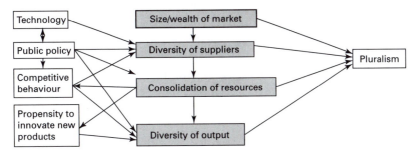

FIGURE 2.1 Determinants of media pluralism

influential factor. But a range of additional elements need to be taken into account when analysing the precise nature of the relationship between media concentrations and pluralism. Each of the other main elements involved is considered more closely below.

## Size/wealth of market

Within any free market economy, the level of resources available for the provision of media will be constrained principally by the size and wealth of that economy, and the propensity of its inhabitants to consume media. The relationship between the size or wealth of a given market and the level of resources which may be tied up in supplying its media seems inescapable, irrespective of which sources of funding are involved. Support for the media through direct payments will be constrained by overall levels of consumer expenditure (itself, a function of the wealth of the economy). The availability of advertising support is also closely related to levels of consumer expenditure or economic wealth in a given market. Even where state intervention supports an 'artificially' high level of indigenous media supply, the level of such support will be a function of the overall wealth of the economy, and of competing 'welfare' claims for public expenditure.

The existence of this relationship between the size and wealth of a market and the level of resources which may be tied up in supplying its media has clear implications for pluralism. Media output may be regarded as a 'public' good, in the sense that it (for example, a radio programme) is generally not destroyed in the act of consumption, and the same unit may be offered to ever wider audiences at low or zero marginal production costs. But, since the majority of costs reside in originating each distinctive unit of media output, the greater the diversity in the composition of output, the greater the resources required. Pluralism depends on the availability of resources to support the origination and distribution of many different sorts of media output. In short, larger and wealthier markets, with greater resources available for the provision of media, can afford a greater diversity of output than smaller markets.

This is clearly reflected in existing patterns of media ownership and output in Europe. The larger and wealthier member states, such as France, Germany, Spain and Italy, can and often do support a greater overall number of suppliers and a greater diversity of media output than smaller or poorer member states such as Ireland, Portugal and Greece. Some counter-examples exist of markets which, although small, nonetheless sustain a diverse provision of media e.g. in northern European and Nordic countries which are characterized by above-average per-capita print media consumption levels (in turn, reflecting wealth, educational and cultural factors). But in general, the smaller scale of resources available for media provision in small peripheral markets makes them prone to concentrations of ownership which, in larger markets, would be deemed unacceptable. Small countries in overlapping language areas (e.g. Switzerland and French-speaking Belgium) are especially prone to market domination by non-indigenous suppliers.

This is not to suggest that large markets avoid the problem of potentially undesirable concentrations of media ownership. Indeed, the wealthier national markets within Europe have supported the development of the vast majority of what are unquestionably the largest and most powerful media conglomerates in Europe, such as News International in the UK, Bertelsmann in Germany, Havas in France or Fininvest in Italy. But, so far as pluralism is concerned, it is not so much the absolute size of media firms (in terms of turnover or profits) that counts as the extent of their domination within particular markets. Large firms will dominate (take a large market share) more easily in small than in large markets. So, the European Union member states with the greatest concentrations of press ownership at present (in terms of shares of national circulations) are Luxembourg and Ireland – both very small markets (Mounier, 1997).

Most of the comparative data currently available concerning national market sizes and levels of diversity in media provision in Europe appears to confirm a generally positive correlation between these variables (Barnard et al., 1996; EIM, 1997; European Audiovisual Observatory, 1997). Analysis of the data submitted by national correspondents to the Council of Europe in 1996 shows that there is a positive correlation between the size of the population in different European countries and the number of daily newspaper titles available in each country (MM-CM, 1997: 16). For magazine publishing, it appears that larger markets are less prone to domination by leading individual publishers than small ones (1997: 18).

International comparisons are more difficult for radio and television broadcasting because the pace of development of commercial broadcasting has varied from country to country, and the diversity of services currently available in each European member state reflects recent technological and regulatory developments as much as economic circumstances. Nonetheless, larger markets such as the UK and France have sufficient audiences and advertising to support a wider diversity of indigenous channels than, say, Ireland or Belgium.

While wealthier markets can afford a more diverse provision, the relationship between market wealth and pluralism is not entirely straightforward. An important intervening variable is the structure of media supply, i.e. how many competing suppliers, as opposed to products, is the market supporting? Within the constraints posed by the overall size and wealth of the market in question, certain industrial configurations would result in a more optimal use of the resources available for media provision than others. Since economies of scale and scope (discussed, in further detail, in Chapter 3) are available to large media firms, it is possible that a more monopolistic industry structure would yield a greater diversity of media output (content) than would be economically feasible in a more fragmented and competitive industry structure. Greater diversity of content is good for pluralism. On the other hand, a monopolistic industry structure poses a threat to pluralism by concentrating more media power into the hands of fewer suppliers.

Large markets can support many media suppliers and the scale of their audiences will be sufficient to encourage strategies of audience segmentation through which many 'minorities' will be supplied with specialized output (although affluent minorities and interest groups will fare best – e.g. the range of subscriber-funded specialist television channels currently available from UK satellite broadcaster BSkyB is heavily weighted towards those audience segments with above-average collective spending power).[1] By contrast, the total resources available for media provision in a small market may be less than those available for even a minority in a larger market. As the given size of a market is reduced, so too will be the economically feasible number of suppliers and the range of audience sub-groups for whom specialized output can be supplied.

For smaller markets, a particular concern is the availability of resources to support indigenous as opposed to less expensive 'imported' content. Ironically, this may lead to a choice between diversity amongst suppliers and diversity of content. If, for example, the cost-efficiencies created through consolidation of domestic media ownership within Scotland were to release resources for an extended range of indigenous Scottish output, then this might seem preferable to a very fragmented ownership structure within Scotland with fewer resources available to devote to the origination of distinctively Scottish media content.

An alternative approach, depending on the economic and political climate of the market in question, might be to sustain pluralism through public subsidies; to inflate the level of resources available for media provision and thereby increase diversity beyond the level which can be afforded 'naturally' in a particular media market.

Variations in the size and wealth of different markets are an awkward challenge for policies intended to secure pluralism. At the level of individual European states, this problem has typically been addressed by the application of different media ownership regulations at the regional/local level from those which apply at the level of the national market. At the pan-European level, no ready solution may be found to the problem of different sizes of national media markets and, as is discussed in Part IV, this represents a continuing obstacle to a harmonized pan-European media ownership policy regime.

Judgements about the respective roles of diverse ownership and diverse content in sustaining pluralism attract greater poignancy in economic circumstances where it seems that only one can be given priority. Small markets often appear to be faced with such a dilemma, and many are dominated by a small number of suppliers, so that the impact of media concentrations on pluralism is a more urgent question. Against this background, the following sections examine the interrelationship of diversity of ownership and heterogeneity of output, and the impact of both on pluralism.

## Diversity of suppliers

The number of separate suppliers in a market is a crucial determinant of pluralism. As levels of media and cross-media ownership become more concentrated, there will be a progressive narrowing of the range of autonomous and independent organizations involved in supplying media. The more powerful individual suppliers become, the greater the potential threat to pluralism.

A distinction may be drawn between ownership of media and control over its content. The extent to which, and the precise point at which, ownership of a media organization will translate into influence over the content of its products has been the subject of analysis, debate and many divided opinions (GAH, 1994). In some cases, regulations create a measure of separation between ownership and editorial control. The content of (particularly broadcast) media may be subject to direct and detailed regulatory prescriptions concerning range and quality, which sorts of input must be included and what steps must be taken to avoid political bias (Gibbons, 1998: 96–7). Alternatively, permission to own certain media products may involve a specific undertaking not to interfere with editorial matters.

Whatever regulatory measures are in place, the opportunities for media owners to assert an indirect influence over the content and the agenda of products they own seem so comprehensive as to defy any absolute guarantees of separation. An owner's influence may manifest itself in the choice of key personnel, or in strategic decisions about which resources to reduce or invest more in, or in arrangements for sourcing or distributing content.

Not all owners wish to exert an influence over the content of their media and, for those that do, the primary motivation may simply be commercial rather than political. Nonetheless, the reason why diversity of ownership is important for pluralism is because media ownership can translate into media power (Meier and Trappel, 1998: 39). Since it is difficult to monitor the intentions of media owners, or to fully regulate their conduct in respect of editorial matters, the single most effective way of ensuring a healthy diversity of voices in the media is to prevent media power from being monopolized – i.e. by ensuring that the supply of media involves a range of autonomous and independent organizations.

Plentiful evidence is available that, in fact, media concentrations do sometimes result in over-representation of those forms of output favoured by dominant media owners. In various editions of *The Media Monopoly*, Bagdikian has revealed how some of the largest US media owners have used their outlets to promote their own values and interests. Similar tendencies can be found right across Europe.

As far as the UK is concerned, some owners of national newspapers have clearly used their titles to further their own political or commercial aims at the expense of balance and responsible journalism (Curran and Seaton, 1997: 72–7). Of course, not all UK newspaper proprietors seek to exert editorial control; for example, the *Guardian* is owned by the Scott Trust which guarantees its editorial independence. However, previous studies have chronicled the tendency of at least some owners – e.g. Victor Matthews (owner of the *Express* titles from 1977 to 1985), Robert Maxwell (owner of the *Mirror* titles from 1984 until 1991) and Rupert Murdoch (current owner of the *Sun*, the *News of the World* and the *Times* titles) – to intervene in editorial decisions in such a way as to dictate and standardize the political line of their newspapers. Editorial interference by owners has frequently been indirect – e.g. through the selection of key personnel, or through the establishment of a culture of obedience and self-censorship – as well as direct – i.e. through literally rewriting editorial leaders.

Research carried out in relation to other European countries such as France, Germany and Italy confirms that the practice of direct and indirect editorial interference by media owners, with detrimental consequences for media diversity, is by no means confined to the newspaper industry nor to UK media proprietors. For example, the tendency of Robert Hersant (owner of the second largest press company in France and with additional media interests in Belgium and elsewhere) to intervene and standardize news and editorial content across many of the titles within his control for political or commercial reasons has been highlighted by several writers (Tunstall and Palmer, 1991: 135–61; Coleridge, 1993: 373–82). In many European Union member states, recent academic work has highlighted some or other form of abuse of the political influence wielded by dominant media corporations, particularly in relation to securing the relaxation of domestic regulatory obstacles to further expansion (Zerdick, 1993; MacLeod, 1996; Humphreys, 1997).

An especially blatant example of the damage which concentrated media ownership may inflict on political pluralism and on democracy more generally is provided by the case of Silvio Berlusconi 'using his three TV stations reaching 40 percent of the Italian audience to give unremitting support to his own political party' in Italy during the March 1994 elections (Graham and Davies, 1997: 32). Subsequent research has revealed 'not only that there was a bigger swing to the right (3.5 percent more) among Berlusconi viewers than the [Italian] electorate in general, but also that this swing could not be explained by the fact that viewers of Berlusconi channels were *already* more right wing. Viewers of these channels were found to be middle of the road and only shifted their voting *after* watching the Berlusconi channels'. The Berlusconi case provides compelling evidence of a causal connection between concentrated media ownership and an undesirable narrowing in the diversity of political opinions available to the public via the media.

Although few instances of concentrated media ownership may give rise to such a manifest abuse of media power, the crucial point remains that greater levels of concentration contribute to a greater risk of media power being abused in this way. Rules to prevent concentrated ownership are an important measure in sustaining media diversity. In some European countries, the approach taken to reducing the risks associated with concentrated ownership involves special safeguards for editorial independence. In Norway, for example, agreements or declarations contracts signed by both editors and owners are used to ensure that owners will not interfere in editorial matters. But, since the possibility of indirect or covert influence by media owners may be as potent a threat for editorial freedom and diversity as that of direct interference in day-to-day editorial decisions, the need for specific restraints on media ownership cannot easily be dismissed.

To the extent that the number of media suppliers provides a proxy for the minimum number of independent voices in a media market, it also represents the most straightforward measure of pluralism. Leaving aside media ownership rules for the moment, the factors influencing the number of media suppliers in a market include – as discussed above – the size of the market (or the level of resources available for media provision), and also the existence of technological or other barriers to market entry.

In recent years, many barriers to entry affecting media markets (e.g. limited spectrum, high initial capital set-up costs) have been overcome by new technology. By and large, regulatory changes affecting media in European member states have sought to accommodate these developments by encouraging new suppliers to enter the market (e.g. through the introduction of additional commercial broadcasting licences). However, market access may also be a function of the competitive behaviour of existing suppliers. Predatory pricing strategies (as may be observed in the newspaper industry) might deter new market entrants or squeeze out existing rivals. Control over important 'gateways' (such as 'electronic programme guides' or EPGs) is another means by which new rivals can be kept out.

Competition, which is a concern in all sectors of business activity, is different from media pluralism and it is dealt with in the following chapter on economic policy aims. However, competition and pluralism are inter-related insofar as anti-competitive behaviour can serve to reduce diversity amongst media suppliers and diversity of content. Notwithstanding special restrictions on media ownership, the prevalence of anti-competitive behaviour may pose an indirect threat by driving out or denying access to other suppliers and output whose presence would increase diversity and pluralism.

But the link between ownership and potential *influence*, which represents a more immediate threat to pluralism, remains the main focus for policies aimed at promoting pluralism. Market size permitting, restrictions on media and cross-media ownership will guarantee the presence of a certain minimum number of separate and autonomous suppliers in the media.

A possible argument against using diverse ownership to secure pluralism is that allowing concentrated ownership may generate cost-efficiencies which would support a greater diversity of content. But if the link between media ownership and potential influence (over public opinion) has been accepted as valid and as a matter of concern for public policy, then it becomes difficult to accept the idea that diversity of ownership should be sacrificed, even in order to secure diversity of output. Additional diversity of content may become economically feasible with concentrated ownership, but it does not stamp out the danger that owners can exert influence over the political agenda of their products. Additional diversity of output cannot counteract the threat to pluralism posed by allowing concentrations of media power.

Thus, diverse ownership remains important for achieving pluralism. Even so, because of the tendency to consolidate editorial resources, different owners cannot be fully equated with different voices. A multiplicity of suppliers is desirable in many ways, but it may not be enough to guarantee an open and diverse system of media provision.

### Consolidation of resources

Pluralism will be affected not only by the level of resources available for media provision in a given market, but also by how these resources are managed. To some extent, how media resources are managed reflects decisions taken at the political level; for example, about what level of media provision should be retained in the public rather than the private sector.

Pluralism will obviously be directly affected by political decisions about the appropriate level of diversity of media ownership and the upper ownership limits which apply. It will also be affected by decisions about the appropriate level of diversity of content which, as discussed above, may sometimes reflect regulatory interventions (particularly in the case of broadcast media).

However, in all European member states, decisions about how media resources will be managed are, in large measure, a matter for the marketplace. The operation of the market may or may not deliver a wide range and diversity of media output. Of crucial relevance is the propensity for consolidation of resources – particularly editorial resources – in 'different' media products. The economic advantages of expansion by media firms (which, naturally, include opportunities to consolidate overlapping resources and cost-functions) are discussed and explained more fully in Part II. For now, we should note that such consolidation has significant implications for pluralism.

This can be demonstrated by looking, first, at the case of monomedia concentrations: concentrations of ownership within any single media sector such as radio or television broadcasting or newspaper publishing. For multi-product television or radio broadcasters, the more homogeneity possible between different services held in common ownership (or the more elements within a programme schedule which can be shared between 'different' stations), the greater the opportunity to reap economies. The same is true for newspaper publishers: common ownership of several titles may facilitate some economizing in the news-gathering process.

Consolidation of editorial functions – or recycling of content amongst different (and possibly overlapping) audience segments – enables media firms to maximize all available economies. However, because patterns of demand tend not to be homogeneous across the market, a tension will exist between the objective of maximizing the available market for the firm's output (through greater product differentiation) and the desire to exhaust any scale economies that are within the firm's control (through greater consolidation). For each product, a judgement will be required as to what level of specialized inputs is sufficient to establish a separate and commercially viable identity within the market. At first glance, the establishment of any 'new' product may appear to promote pluralism. But, if the new product involves the incorporation of only a few specialized inputs into a standard basic product, then its arrival may contribute to standardization of media output rather than to increased diversity.

So, a key aspect of the relationship between media concentrations and pluralism is the extent to which concentrated ownership encourages consolidation of cost functions – especially editorial – between what are ostensibly 'rival' products held in common ownership. But, even *without* common ownership, some cost-sharing is possible between rival media products and this may also have an impact on pluralism. For example, radio or television broadcast services which are separately owned may share elements of content, whether through joint purchasing of programmes, networking arrangements or secondary trading in transmitted output.

For rival newspaper publishers, collective economies can also be exploited through sharing or contracting out to third parties activities such as distribution or printing. As far as pluralism is concerned, the main issue is whether cost-sharing between rival newspaper publishers extends to deriving their journalistic input from the same sources, or from each other. If many independent suppliers are 'originating' their news stories from a common source (such as a particular newswire service), then there is cause for concern about journalistic diversity and about the scope for independence in agenda setting.

The UK national newspaper market provides several examples of multi-product firms all of whom benefit from economies of scope, but only some of these economies reflect shared journalistic and editorial resources. More significantly, all UK newspaper suppliers outsource a portion of their news content from external news-gathering services. In many cases, rival newspaper publishers are using the same agencies, i.e. PA, AFP or Reuters. Many national and regional UK newspaper publishers are also major shareholders in PA (the Press Association), one of the most widely used commercial news-supply agencies. News-gathering services such as PA not only provide rival newspapers with the same 'original' stories, they also, in some cases, provide full page layouts with recycled content customized for the title in question.

The practice of recycling news content is by no means confined to the UK but is commonplace in many other European countries, including Belgium, Cyprus, Italy, Poland, Switzerland and Sweden. In Belgium, because national newspapers lack their own dedicated correspondents for international stories, there is a tendency for all titles to use exactly the same news agencies and sources of content. The tendency for the same content to reappear in 'rival' media products is sometimes encouraged by interconnected ownership of these products but it may also occur when 'rival' products are controlled by entirely separate owners. So, even where a number of rival media owners are involved in supplying media, this will not provide an absolute guarantee of editorial diversity between their products.

As with monomedia concentrations, the implications of cross-media ownership for pluralism depend, at least partly, on whether such cross-ownership encourages consolidation of editorial functions or recycling of product content. To the extent that the same content and editorial approach may be embodied in 'different' media products held under common ownership, then cross-ownership of the media will have a negative impact on pluralism.

Cross-ownership provides opportunities for cross-promotion of commonly owned products. The impact of cross-promotion on pluralism depends on whether it is used by media owners simply to strengthen the market share of existing media products (in which case it will have a negative impact on diversity) or whether cross-promotion is used to support *de novo* product innovation, thus extending the range of existing products in the market.

## Diversity of output

Diversity in the content of media represents a central aspect of political and cultural pluralism. Diverse ownership will contribute to a diversity in output so long as separate ownership discourages consolidation or sharing of editorial functions or content between owners of 'rival' products. In practice, such cost-sharing may be more feasible and more typical where different products are held in common ownership. To the extent that this is so, restrictions on concentrations of media ownership serve to promote diversity of output. However, separate ownership cannot guarantee that elements of the same output or the same agenda will not be shared by rival owners' products.

Furthermore, it is possible that concentrations of media and cross-media ownership may actually have a positive impact on diversity of output; for example, if the scale of the resources available to a large firm enables it to support or cross-subsidize a loss-making product. Assuming that commercial firms in the media, as in any other sector, are primarily interested in maximizing profits, then the clearest motivation for investing in loss-making products would be the hope of eventually making them profitable. (An alternative motivation – referred to as 'brand proliferation' – is to diversify and occupy all market niches, so as to deter market entry on the part of other potential suppliers; such a strategy clearly has negative implications for pluralism). Large media firms may be better equipped than their smaller rivals to withstand the financial risks associated with deficit-funding a temporarily loss-making product. The survival of such a product might or might not be regarded as a bonus for diversity.

Because of the cost-efficiencies and the scale of resources available to large media firms, such dominant players are often thought to be better equipped than their smaller competitors to invest in the development of new products. Similarly, firms whose activities are diversified across many different sectors of the media may be in a better position to innovate new multimedia products than their monomedia rivals. The additional capital and the mix of expertise available to large, diversified media conglomerates are advantages which, in theory, ought to enable such firms to innovate new products (and contribute to diversity) more readily than their smaller rivals.

On the other hand, it may be argued that many of the opportunities for new product innovation in the media industry of the 21st century do not require extensive initial capital investment. Also, even if larger media organizations have greater resources for investment, they do not necessarily engender a creative or risk-taking management culture. In fact, as media organizations grow larger they often have less flexibility and may exhibit a reduced propensity for entrepreneurship.

The extent to which monopolistic ownership structures are conducive to product innovation and diversity of output is, therefore, not an entirely straightforward issue. More generally, in circumstances where enlargement and cross-sectoral ownership give rise to economies of scale and scope (without introducing uniformity or standardization of content), it cannot be assumed that cost savings will be reinvested in additional media products rather than divested elsewhere or simply returned to shareholders.

Since the relationship between diverse ownership and diversity of output is, in some sense, an ambiguous one, restrictions on ownership may not be enough to guarantee diversity of output. Other policy instruments are available and have often been used in conjunction with media ownership restrictions in order to encourage plurality within the supply of media. For example, the range and diversity of output embodied in a particular media product or service may be subject to special regulatory requirements. In addition, support for 'public service' broadcasting (PSB) services (for which diversity of content and political impartiality are standard requirements) will contribute directly to diversity and pluralism in media provision.

## Implications for public policy

The main concern associated with excessive media concentrations is pluralism. Concentrations of media ownership can lead to over-representation of certain political opinions or forms of cultural output (those favoured by powerful media owners, whether on commercial or ideological grounds) and to exclusion of others. The *risk* that concentrated media power may create such imbalances – and the accompanying risks for democracy and for social cohesion – represents a key concern for policy-making, irrespective of whether proof can be established that all large media owners actually intend to ensure the predominance of certain forms of output.

As a consequence, rules which limit media and cross-media ownership are generally seen as an essential means of sustaining and promoting pluralism. Restrictions on media ownership provide a way of rationing power over which ideas will circulate (or not circulate) in the public domain. To avoid allowing such power to fall into the hands of too few individuals or corporations, virtually all countries in Europe have adopted some special rules which restrict ownership of the media.

However, the cause-and-effect relationship between media concentrations and pluralism is anything but straightforward. The level of pluralism that exists in any market depends not only on diversity of ownership but on a range of other interrelated variables. So, in order to achieve pluralism, an array of policy tools other than media ownership restrictions may also need to be brought into play.

The diversity of media suppliers in a market is, in turn, affected by issues such as the wealth of the market (or how many suppliers it can support) and the state of technology (what methods of distribution are accessible). In markets that are not large enough to support several separate suppliers, a strong case may be argued in favour of using public subsidies to extend diversity of media ownership. Many European countries provide grants or subsidies which extend the range of newspapers and broadcast services available to the public. For example, the UK Treasury provides a substantial annual grant for Gaelic television programming in Scotland and a major grant for S4C, a Welsh-language television service transmitted in Wales. Subsidies aimed at public service broadcasters may prove especially effective in promoting pluralism because of the general commitment of PSB organizations to principles of universal access, impartiality and so on.

In addition to diverse media ownership, the other principal determinant of media pluralism is diversity of content. The development of large media groups, if left unregulated, might possibly contribute to a wider range of products. On the other hand, economic motivations may sometimes exert a standardising influence over the output of large media firms. Media and cross-media ownership rules will protect diversity of content, but only to the extent that diverse ownership impedes the consolidation of journalistic resources and editorial functions between products owned by rival proprietors. However, rival proprietors may sometimes seek to reduce costs by sharing editorial content. For example, the reliance of separate newspaper publishers on the same 'external' news-gathering agencies means that a news story can be investigated only once but reported several times over, using the same journalistic input but (perhaps) a different editorial slant, in several 'rival' titles. The cost-savings shared by all of the publishers come at some expense to pluralism. But this situation prevails because the policy instruments intended to preserve pluralism are generally aimed at diversity amongst distributors (i.e. newspaper publishers, television and radio broadcasters) rather than diversity in what is supplied.

The traditional design of media ownership policy has tended to overlook the potential for monopolized control at earlier or later stages in the vertical supply chain for media. Monopolistic tendencies in 'upstream' phases (e.g. news gathering) or in 'downstream' phases (e.g. the new so-called gateways in broadcasting represented by conditional access systems or electronic programme guides) may well serve to narrow and inhibit media pluralism. Competition-based regulation provides a means of checking the behaviour of such monopolists. Those who control resources or functions considered essential for all potential market participants may be required, under competition law, to provide rivals with access to such resources on 'fair' terms. But pluralism, as a distinct policy objective, requires its own additional measures to sustain an open and diverse system of media provision.

Although diverse ownership of broadcasting and the press will not necessarily guarantee diversity of media output, the existence of a diversity of media owners should contribute positively to pluralism. Even if all owners choose to rely on or share many sources of content, their rivalry will promote a culture of dissent which is healthy for democracy. Most importantly, diverse ownership will prevent any single supplier from having absolute control over the agenda and will therefore reduce the scope for potentially dangerous abuses of public or political influence.

So, in order to secure pluralism, rules which constrain concentrations of media and cross-media ownership remain indispensable. As well as using policy instruments to promote diverse ownership, pluralism will be strengthened by policies which encourage diversity of content. Regulators in some European countries and in the US have, at one time or another, introduced rules which oblige dominant television broadcasters to source a minimum proportion of their broadcast output from programme producers who are 'independent', separate or autonomous entities. Such measures (for example, in the UK, a 25 per cent compulsory access quota on ITV and the BBC for independent producers) are effective in extending the range of voices reflected within media content.

But direct interventions or prescriptions intended to promote diversity of content raise the problem of unwelcome intrusions on press freedom. Standardization of media content is undesirable but so, too, is state interference in editorial decision-making. The same problem applies to management strategies involving consolidation of editorial resources and functions for which there may be a compelling commercial logic. Such strategies may be damaging for pluralism but interventions to counteract them are difficult either to frame or to implement, since the principle of press freedom is not easily separated from the freedom of media firms to manage their editorial resources as they see fit.

When it comes to broadcasting, policy-makers in many countries have often been prepared to put the principle of 'perceived viewer welfare' ahead of the principle of press freedom. The approaches taken to promote plurality of content on broadcast media include imposing obligations to provide a diversity of types of programming and/or imposing a duty of impartiality on broadcasters (i.e. requiring a balance and diversity of viewpoints to be conveyed on all important issues). Across Europe, such duties have readily been imposed on commercial as well as public service broadcasters.

Newspapers, on the other hand, are rarely subjected to overt content regulation. Measures aimed at separating ownership from editorial control represent a valuable alternative approach to maintaining diversity of content in the newspaper sector. Many European countries, including Norway, Portugal and the Netherlands, use 'editorial agreements' to achieve such a separation. Editorial agreements may be voluntary or statutory and involve a written statement which guarantees the rights of editors to shape the content of their products free from interference by media owners. Some editorial agreements go so far as to create rights for editorial staff to participate in and veto appointments of new personnel.

In summary, media ownership rules that ensure a reasonable diversity of commercial players are a crucial means of promoting a diverse system of media provision. However, ownership rules alone are not always sufficient to guarantee pluralism and they need to be backed up, as appropriate, by such additional policy measures as those mentioned above.

## Notes

1. According to BSkyB, 'only 14 per cent of Sky subscribers are over 55 versus 28 per cent in the population as a whole. As a result, satellite and cable owners are 20 per cent more likely to be in full-time employment' (BSkyB, 1996: 39).

# 3

# Industrial and Economic Policy Aims

The media is a significant sector of economic activity, accounting for some 3–5 per cent of Gross Domestic Product (GDP) in most countries of Western Europe. The performance of this economically valuable sector is, to some extent at least, tied up with the market structures in which media firms operate and, especially, with degrees of concentration of ownership. Thus, instances of market dominance in the media raise concern not only about pluralism but also about the economic well-being and performance of the media industry.

This chapter introduces the main economic policy issues associated with concentrations of media ownership. The economic consequences of allowing media and cross-media empires to develop depend on how such ownership patterns affect the behaviour and the performance of media firms.

The trends towards concentrated ownership discussed earlier reflect the special attractions, for media firms, of engaging in various strategies of expansion. In theory, the main advantages surrounding horizontal, vertical and diagonal growth tend to centre on increased 'efficiency' or on increased 'market power' (George et al., 1992: 63–4; Martin, 1993: 258–82). The main benefits, in practice, of monomedia (horizontal) and cross-media (vertical or diagonal) expansion strategies are explored in further empirical detail in Chapters 4 and 5, and sometimes include a variety of interesting and alternative strategic and managerial sub-goals not directly accounted for by profit maximization.

Generally speaking, however, industrial economics attributes expansion – whether horizontal, vertical or diagonal and whether through internal growth or through mergers and takeovers – to two key incentives associated with profit-maximizing behaviour. From the firm's point of view, the main benefits of expansion are that it may increase market power (i.e. the ability to control prices, output, etc.) or it may increase efficiency. As far as the collective economic welfare of society is concerned, the overall impact of firms' growth strategies depends on what balance is achieved between these two possible outcomes. Efficiency gains that allow for an improved use of society's resources are beneficial to the economy as a whole. On the other hand, increased market power in the hands of individual firms poses a threat to rivals and consumers and is recognized as damaging to the public interest.

Economic policy-makers are sometimes confronted by the problem that proposed mergers and expansion strategies may result in *both* outcomes. For example, as a media firm enlarges, it may well be able to exploit greater economies of scale and economies of scope, thus allowing for a more productive use of resources. So, consolidation appears to be warranted and desirable on the grounds of increased efficiency. At the same time, however, the greater market power associated with increased size might create new opportunities for the enlarged media firm to raise prices or otherwise abuse its dominant market position. Although enlargement may, in the first place, have been predicated on improvements in efficiency (e.g. the realization of economies of scale), it might well then be accompanied by the accumulation of a dominant market position which, in turn, can lead to behaviour and practices that run contrary to the public interest (Moschandreas, 1994: 483). Once a firm achieves a dominant position, the removal of competitive pressures may give rise to various inefficiencies, including excessive expenditure of resources aimed simply at maintaining dominance.

So, a major economic concern associated with concentrated media ownership is its impact on competition. Competition is generally regarded as an essential means of fostering economic efficiency and of averting abusive behaviour by dominant firms. In essence, competition – the presence of several competing suppliers – helps to ensure that firms keep their costs and prices down, which encourages a more efficient use of resources (Scherer and Ross, 1990: 20). If there are few or no rivals in a market, then suppliers can more easily get away with offering goods and services that are costly or inferior. Competitive pressures incentivize managers to improve the performance of their firm relative to rivals and this, in turn, benefits consumers and society at large. Monopolists – whether in the media or in other sectors – are usually seen as less efficient than competitive firms. Monopolists may suppress new innovatory products and may, sometimes, engage in 'unfair' competition.

On the other hand, a media industry in which ownership is too fragmented is also susceptible to inefficiency. It is often argued that, because of the availability of economies of scale in the media, large firms are needed in order to ensure the most cost-effective possible use of resources. So, if promoting cost-efficiency in the media industry is regarded as the dominant policy objective, then encouraging greater concentration of media ownership may be consistent with the public interest.

In short, the need to sustain competition and the desire to maximize efficiency are the two main economic policy goals affected by concentrations of media ownership. These goals are related, in that fair and plentiful competition is seen as an essential means of sustaining efficiency. But the two objectives may pull in opposite directions. If, because of the availability of economies of scale, the optimal size of a firm in some media markets is so large as to preclude rivals, then a trade-off will occur between encouraging more competition and achieving maximum efficiency gains.

## Promoting competition

The word 'monopoly' comes from the Greek words for 'single seller'. According to Adam Smith, when market forces are thwarted by monopoly, so too will be the tendency for resources to be allocated in the manner 'most agreeable to the interests of the whole society' (1937: 594–5). The issue of how competitive markets work to allocate resources has been developed considerably by economists since Smith's time.

One of the main concerns associated with allowing individual firms to establish dominance in particular markets is that they may charge prices that are too high and become careless about their costs (Scherer and Ross, 1990: 19–23). Monopolists may become complacent about product quality and about the need to innovate, to the detriment of consumers. Another important worry is that dominant firms will 'waste' too much of their resources in activities designed to maintain their market dominance. They may engage in business practices that are intended to squeeze rivals out the market or to deter new rivals (offering products which consumers may want) from entering.

Conventional economic theory suggests that 'perfect competition' (i.e. the existence of many suppliers, in open markets, offering homogeneous products to buyers who have perfect knowledge of all available substitutes) is one route towards bringing about an efficient allocation of resources. But, in the real world, there are few if any examples of perfect competition. Instead, very many markets in modern industrialized economies are dominated by a small number of large firms who have some degree of market power. The potential for this market power to be abused, and to result in a misallocation of resources, is the main economic rationale underlying competition policy (George et al., 1992: 314).

The media industry is prone to oligopoly and, in turn, to such resource misallocation. In the UK, for example, very high inflation in prices charged for television advertising during the 1980s can be associated with monopolized control of commercial airtime during this period. More recently, the potential for abuse of market power wielded by 'gatekeeper' monopolists in broadcasting – i.e. those with control over important gateways between content suppliers and viewers such as owners of pre-dominant systems of conditional access (CAS) or electronic programme guides – has raised many concerns (Cowie, 1997). In addition, the price war which has affected UK national daily newspaper markets since 1993 provides an example of how dominant media suppliers may use their strength and resources to reinforce and extend positions of market dominance.

The standard provisions of national and European competition law apply to all sectors of industry including media (though public service broadcasters are often exempted). Competition policy has traditionally worked on the assumption that the efficiency of markets depends directly on their competitive structure and, especially, on the extent of seller concentration. So, competition policy may sometimes involve 'structural' interventions – attempts to bring about market structures which are less concentrated – on the assumption that this will ensure good behaviour by competing firms and promote improved industrial performance (Moschandreas, 1994: 482).

Upper restrictions on levels of media ownership represent a means of structural intervention through which competition amongst media can be promoted and seller concentration can be avoided. Special restrictions on media ownership are a common feature in most European countries and elsewhere, but they usually owe their existence to concerns about pluralism and not competition. Media ownership restrictions are generally intended to protect political and cultural pluralism which, as a policy objective, is quite different from promoting competition. Nonetheless, ownership limits intended to preserve pluralism may, at the same time, also serve to prevent the development and subsequent possible abuses of excessive market power by dominant media firms.

However, the use of ownership rules to alter the structure of a market is what some economists would consider to be a fairly extreme form of intervention. In recent years, the emphasis of competition policy has shifted away from such structural interventions towards alternative 'behavioural' measures which regulate the conduct of dominant firms in such a way as to ensure that market power is not abused. In the UK, the 1998

Competition Act has brought the UK approach more into line with that of the European Union, where the focus is on remedies to anti-competitive behaviour rather than on corporate structures (Feintuck, 1999: 91).

The change in emphasis from structural to behavioural regulation reflects major theoretical developments in the area of industrial organization over recent decades. It is now widely recognized that what matters for efficiency is not necessarily the number of rival suppliers that exist in a market *per se* but whether competitive pressure from incumbent or even potential market entrants is sufficient to induce firms to operate efficiently and to deter anti-competitive behaviour (Moschandreas, 1994: 484).

So, when interventions are called for to promote competition, ownership restrictions offer one possibility and regulation aimed at encouraging monopolistic firms into behaviour consistent with the public interest offers another. The latter approach holds out advantages in circumstances where monopolistic ownership is considered inevitable, for example, in the case of 'natural' monopoly. 'A natural monopoly arises when technology is such that economies of scale exist which are exhausted at a scale of operation which is so large in relation to the market that only one firm can operate efficiently' (ibid.: 485). Where there is room in the market for only one supplier, or just a few suppliers (a 'natural oligopoly'), this implies that increased competition would result in higher costs and less efficiency.

Many sub-sectors of the media have some natural monopoly or natural oligopoly characteristics. The prevalence of both economies of scale and scope means that joint production – i.e. production within one firm – of a set of media outputs may well be demonstrably cheaper than their production by a multitude of separate firms. This situation presents a dilemma for policy-making. Whereas competition is generally seen as an essential stimulus to efficiency, the counter-argument may be mounted that ownership ceilings which promote competition result in an economic welfare loss by stopping media firms from realizing all available economies of scale and scope.

Yet even when securing diversity of ownership involves sacrificing some potential efficiency gains, the advantages of having more than one supplier are often considered to take precedence. In the UK, the general approach towards regulation of so-called natural monopolies such as gas, electricity and telephony has changed markedly since the 1980s (George et al., 1992: 340). The postwar policy of exclusive public ownership of such activities has been reversed via a programme of privatization, regulation and efforts to promote competition. This new approach to 'the natural monopoly problem' highlights the perceived importance of introducing competitive pressures into industries that are prone to monopoly wherever this is feasible and whether or not it involves the loss of some potential efficiency gains (1992: 361).

## Monopolies and technological change

One of the most difficult challenges for media policy-makers in recent years has been that of how to deal with monopolies during periods of rapid technological change. The growth of the Internet and of 'new' media has been the catalyst for a great many mergers and alliances which have taken place since the late 1990s. Many large scale deals such as the AOL/Time Warner merger or the acquisition of Endemol by Telefónica, both in 2000, have emphasized the perceived importance of developing market power across all major stages in the vertical supply chain. This has raised concern about bottlenecks, gateway monopolies and control over access to new media. According to Hughes, 'the strategic ambition of most of these players is to create vertically integrated businesses that control the gateways across TV, phone and wireless networks, offering customers a single bill, a single brand and a single EPG' (2000: 37).

The problem with monopolized control of new phases in the supply chain for media – e.g. conditional access systems, subscriber management systems (SMSs) or electronic programme guides – is that these functions are often located centrally between new service providers and viewers and so they occupy what is potentially a very powerful position. When individual firms have exclusive control over a vital activity or piece of infrastructure that all media suppliers need in order to reach viewers or to collect charges then, because of their control of the bottleneck, these firms are in a position to act as 'gatekeepers' and to decide who may or may not be allowed market access. This has important implications for the public interest. Gatekeepers are often vertically integrated firms that not only control the 'gateway' in question but also have an involvement in upstream and downstream activities. The problem is that vertically integrated gatekeepers have both the means and the incentive to favour their own services and to exclude rivals. Gateway monopolists can abuse their position either by denying access to rival service providers or by offering access on terms that are very disadvantageous to potential competitors. Like monopolists in any other situation, gatekeepers have the power to raise prices, restrict output and engage in other forms of behaviour that run contrary to the interests of consumers.

The relationship between monopoly and technological innovation is not altogether straightforward. Whereas some economists believe that monopolists tend to suppress the rate of new product innovation, others (following on from Schumpeter) take the view that 'firms need protection from competition before they will bear the risks and costs of invention' and so monopoly offers the ideal situation for innovation (Scherer and Ross, 1990: 31). Schumpeter put forward the argument that the incentive of being able to reap monopoly profits, at least in the short term, is absolutely vital in encouraging firms to innovate and thus in stimulating overall economic growth and technological progress.

Much of the investment in new media products and new avenues for distribution of media output, not only in the UK but elsewhere, has come from existing large players in the media and communications industries, such as Time Warner, Pearson, Bertelsmann, BT and Telefónica. This has resulted in some cases in the emergence of *de facto* vertical and horizontal monopolies. In the UK, BSkyB's control over the prevalent conditional access technology for pay-TV and its dominant position as a supplier in the market for pay-TV programming have been subject to investigation by the competition authorities in recent years.

In discussing the problems posed by regulation of gateway monopolies, Collins and Murroni point out that 'the characteristic regulatory response of imposing structural constraints on dominant firms is often at odds with the need to allow firms to find their own shape during phases of transformation' (1996: 37). The high cost of activities such as laying broadband cable infrastructures or developing conditional access systems often militates against duplication by rivals, at least in the short term. Thus, structural interventions to prevent monopolized ownership of new technologies may have the unwelcome outcome of simply choking off rates of investment and innovation.

This implies that, in order to encourage the development of new media, monopolies may have to be tolerated, at least in the short term, and their conduct regulated in such a way as to prevent anti-competitive behaviour. For some, the best response in a situation of dynamic technological change is to regulate behaviour to ensure that monopoly power is not abused (ibid.). If implemented effectively, the requirement that gateway monopolists provide third-party access (for rivals to their vital facilities) on fair and non-discriminatory terms will help to promote wider market access. Under European competition law, natural monopoly bottlenecks are usually dealt with in this way under what is known as the 'essential facilities' doctrine which places a duty on monopolists to facilitate market access for rivals on fair and equal terms (Cowie, 1997).

The close interdependence between access to media content and access to distribution infrastructures has led to numerous calls for strengthened policies to tackle vertical cross-ownership. Oliver has suggested that the monopolized control of content (e.g. sports rights, movies etc.) needed to encourage consumer take-up of new distribution systems is 'creating bottlenecks and allowing system owners to control and restrict consumer choice' (2000: 64). Likewise, Shooshan and Cave express concern that 'there is a real risk viewpoint diversity will be diminished if firms with market power in distribution are allowed to extend their dominance into content/ software' (2000: 12). Some favour restrictions on cross-ownership between distribution activities and those that confer gatekeeping powers. Others are concerned about the need to avoid stifling innovation by introducing too much regulation. Most, however, emphasize the need for regulators to enforce open standards and procedures that allow interconnection and interoperability between rival technologies and that safeguard access points to the media for suppliers that are independent and unaffiliated.

Regulation of technical standards (to ensure open access) and close supervision of the behaviour of dominant players are important means of avoiding problems that arise from bottlenecks and gateway monopolies. They cannot, however, guarantee to eliminate all inefficiencies associated with market dominance. The exercise of dominance across the supply chain for media does not simply imply the possibility of unfair pricing, vertical restraints and other restrictive practices which run contrary to public welfare. It may also involve an excessive expenditure of resources in order to gain strategic advantages over existing or potential competitors. A range of other inefficiencies, sometimes referred to as 'X-inefficiencies', may set in because of the adverse affect on managerial incentives and controls caused by lack of competitive pressure.

## Promoting efficiency

Effective competition, involving many rather than just one or two rival suppliers, is clearly an ideal way to avoid the substantial range of economic deficiencies associated with excessive market dominance. To that end, the imposition of upper limits on media or cross-media ownership seems to offer useful safeguards for the process of competition and for the interests of media consumers. However, restrictions on media ownership also play a role in determining whether or not firms are allowed to reach their 'optimal' size and corporate configuration. Because of the economic characteristics of media, strategies of expansion within and across media industries *do*, in fact, quite often allow firms to make better use of the resources available for media provision. The fact that expansion gives rise to efficiency gains provides a compelling public interest case in favour of media ownership policies which encourage rather than curb such growth strategies.

To analyse what sorts of efficiency gains are available, it is helpful to consider once again each of the main types of concentration strategy – horizontal, vertical and diagonal – in turn. 'Horizontal' or monomedia concentrations means concentrated ownership within the same single sector of media activity (e.g. radio broadcasting or magazine publishing). Cross-media concentrations may involve either vertical or diagonal cross-ownership or both. 'Vertical' concentration refers to cross-ownership of activities usually within the same sector but which span two or more different stages in the vertical supply chain (e.g. cross-ownership of television programme-making plus television broadcasting activities). 'Diagonal' or conglomerate cross-ownership refers to combined ownership of activities in several different areas of the media (e.g. radio broadcasting plus magazine publishing plus newspaper publishing).

Looking, first, at monomedia or horizontal growth – i.e. expanding the firm's market share either through internal growth or, particularly, by acquisition of another firm with a similar product – potential efficiency gains undoubtedly serve as an important incentive for expansion. The relationship between the size and efficiency of firms depends largely on the availability of economies of scale – i.e. whether marginal costs are less than average costs as output expands – which, in turn, is often determined by technological considerations. When marginal costs are less than average costs – as, indeed, is the case in very many sectors of the media – horizontal expansion will create economies of scale.

Economies of scale, then, are the main economic motive for horizontal mergers or acquisitions in the media industry. Economies of scale are prevalent in the media because, in general, the business of supplying media is characterized by high initial production costs but very low or minimal marginal distribution costs. So, concentrated media firms that can spread production costs across ever-larger audiences will benefit from diminishing per viewer (or per reader) costs as consumption expands.

The potential efficiency gains arising from concentrated ownership do not necessarily end there. The realisation of scale economies may (arguably), in turn, facilitate higher levels of gross investment and speedier adoption of new technologies. Faster-growing firms may attract better-quality personnel (George et al., 1992: 63). Internal growth may have been motivated by the existence of unused resources (e.g. surplus printing or production capacity) within the firm or, by the same token, horizontal expansion may create the opportunity for cost-reductions through elimination of overlapping or excess capacity (Martin, 1993: 266). In theory, efficiency gains of this sort represent a benefit not only for the firm but also for society at large.

As far as vertical concentrations are concerned – i.e. cross-ownership of more than one stage in the production and supply chain – an important consideration in terms of efficiency is the difference between the expenses involved in buying from or selling to other firms – obtaining information, negotiating contracts, etc. – and, alternatively, the expenses involved in carrying out the functions performed by these other firms within one's own organization. Ronald Coase (1937) first introduced the idea that 'the market' and 'the firm' represent *alternative* modes for allocating resources. For Coase, firms exist because the co-ordination of economic activity through the firm (by hierarchies of managers) is less costly than through the market (by the pricing system). Integration of activities within the structure of a firm will occur because it creates transaction cost savings.

Coase's central notion that the *raison d'être* for firms is efficiency gains has been widely accepted and Oliver Williamson's work has built upon this idea to develop the concept of transaction costs and their significance for the choice of organizational form. The potential for cost reduction within a firm may stem from improved information – e.g. about price or product specifications or, more generally, about the market – or from eliminating opportunistic behaviour (Williamson and Winter, 1993: 92). If transactions carried out in the market which are at different vertical stages are characterized by uncertainty, or if they occur frequently, or if there is a high degree of asset specificity, then there will be efficiency motives for a vertically integrated organizational form to develop (George et al., 1992: 63).

However, vertical integration may also offer valuable strategic advantages (Martin, 1993: 273). Integrated firms can avoid the market power of dominant suppliers or buyers – vertical expansion gives secure access to, for example, essential inputs or distribution outlets for output. This is a key advantage in the media, since firms depend on secure access both to content and to avenues for distribution of content. But it is sometimes difficult to disentangle the pursuit of greater efficiency and greater security from the pursuit of monopoly power (George et al., 1992: 72). Vertical expansion could disadvantage rivals by giving the integrated firm control over all substitute inputs at an upstream stage (e.g. a broadcaster acquiring all producers of, say, football programming). Vertical integration may protect the market power of incumbent firms by increasing barriers to entry (George et al., 1992: 64). 'A firm that controls high-quality supplies of an essential input will enjoy a cost advantage *vis-à-vis* less fortunate rivals' (Martin, 1993: 274). Thus, a vertically integrated organizational form can be seen, in one sense (that of Coase), as a *response* to market failures and imperfections and, in another sense, as the *source* of such market imperfections.

Turning to diagonal expansion – i.e. across different product markets (e.g. newspapers plus television broadcasting) – industrial economists have suggested a range of possible efficiency motives. It is not always easy to draw a sharp distinction between what is horizontal and what is diagonal expansion, because the distinction between product markets is not always clear, especially in the case of 'converging' sectors of the media. Either way – whether a firm is expanding horizontally into the production of a different variety of the *same* product, or whether it is expanding diagonally into the production of a *different* product – a useful potential efficiency gain is the opportunity to share the use of specialized resources or expertise across more than one product (Martin, 1993: 279).

Efficiency gains would arise if specialist content gathered for one media product (e.g. a newspaper or magazine) can be easily and cheaply reformatted into another (e.g. an electronic newsletter). Economies of scope will be present if the cost of producing two non-identical products under common ownership is lower than if each were produced by separate firms (Moschandreas, 1994: 150) – for example, because both products share some component. '[T]he more closely products are related in either production or distribution, the more important will be economies of scope which make it cheaper for several products to be manufactured and/or distributed by the same firm rather than separately in different firms' (George et al., 1992: 82).

According to Douglas Gomery, the tendency towards expansion and concentration in the media reflects the fact that 'the optimal market for selling a television programme, a feature film, music on CD or tape, or a printed publication is the entire planet' (1993: 64). Diversification from one media activity into another (diagonal expansion) allows firms the advantage of spreading the risk of innovating media products across a variety of formats or delivery methods (ibid.: 66).

Alan Albarran and John Dimmick have suggested the concept of 'economies of multiformity' as a way of describing the efficiency gains resulting from cross-sectoral (as opposed to horizontal) expansion in the media. This term refers to whatever cost-savings and/ or revenue gains may arise when communication firms extend their activities across two or more sectors (Albarran and Dimmick, 1996: 43). For example, economies of multiformity may arise because cross-sectoral diversification allows for increased usage of an existing infrastructure (e.g. offering telephony as well as television services over the same cable distribution system), or when existing media content can be reformatted into different products at a low marginal cost, or because additional outlets are gained through which some key ingredient of media content which has already been contracted can then be further exploited.

## Implications for public policy

The availability of a range of potential efficiency gains as media firms expand and diversify suggests that the design of media and cross-media ownership policies will have important economic consequences. Ownership policies determine whether or not firms operating in the media industry are allowed to reach the size and corporate structure most conducive to exploiting economies of scale and scope. A strong economic case can be made in favour of encouraging firms to exploit all such economies to the full, so that unnecessary waste can be eliminated and the resources available for media provision can be used to best effect.

However, the concept of industrial efficiency is not just about minimizing costs. Efficiency has been defined as 'a maximum value of outputs for given values of inputs' (Shepherd, 1979: 32). The 'value' to society of different sorts of media outputs is notoriously difficult to measure, which makes analysis of efficiency difficult to carry out in the context of media. Nonetheless, efficiency implies producing output of the right quality and quantity to satisfy the needs and wants of society. Product diversity represents one aspect of quality. To the extent that diversity of media output is of greater 'value' to society than uniformity, then some duplication of media production resources need be seen not as wasteful but as contributing to efficiency.

But the theoretical case to suggest improved economic efficiency for firms who, in circumstances of unregulated ownership, are able to maximize economies of scale and scope, tends to be well supported in literature. Highly concentrated media firms who can spread production costs across wider product and geographic markets will clearly benefit from natural economies of scale in the media (Gomery, 1993: 64–5). In addition, 'the potential for stitching together media businesses to create a fully integrated corporation – from making the product to selling it in more and more markets to controlling the very outlets from which customers buy or rent – offers the vertically integrated corporation significant economic advantages' (ibid.).

The fact that large media firms who can capitalise on natural economies of scale and scope or other size advantages ought to enjoy a better financial performance than those who cannot is not the only economic issue that policy-makers need to take into account. Notwithstanding the potential efficiency gains which motivate firms to acquire market dominance, the detrimental effects on competition which may accompany excessive concentration are a powerful countervailing concern for industrial policy-making.

This holds true for media as much as for other sectors of industry. Although strategies of expansion and concentration may be predicated on achieving improvements in efficiency (e.g. greater economies of scale), they might equally reflect a desire to accumulate and exploit market power (e.g. to profit from increased negotiating leverage in the market for advertiser access to audiences). The problem remains that once a dominant position has been achieved, whether incidentally or by deliberate design, the removal of competitive pressures may pave the way for internal inefficiency or slack and can lead to 'anti-competitive' behaviour and practices which run counter to the public interest.

So, if media ownership policy were determined solely on the basis of economic considerations, the main challenge for policy-makers would be to decide how best, in an industry strongly characterized by economies of scale and scope and by tendencies towards oligopoly, to weigh up potential efficiency losses caused by diverse ownership against the benefits of sustaining effective levels of competition. In reality, competition and efficiency are not the main concerns underlying media ownership policy. Special policies to deal with ownership of the media owe their existence, in the first place, to concerns about *pluralism*, not economics. Even so, economic arguments have gained steadily and substantially greater importance in debates about media ownership policy in recent years.

In order to fully evaluate concerns about the economic opportunity costs involved in restricting ownership of the media, it is necessary to investigate, in closer detail, the relationship between media ownership restrictions and the performance of the media. Part II presents the findings of recent empirical research into how and why firms in the UK media sector benefit economically and financially from strategies of monomedia and cross-media expansion.

# Economics of Media
# Concentrations

# 4

# Monomedia Expansion

It is widely assumed that large and diversified media firms are more efficient than smaller ones. This assumption has been central to the industrial case, argued successfully in many European countries over recent years, in favour of liberalizing media ownership policies. But relatively little research has been dedicated to investigating exactly what gains arise when media firms embark on strategies of enlargement and cross-sectoral expansion. This chapter and the next are devoted to examining the economic implications of concentrated media ownership. They investigate the extent to which strategies of expansion by media firms may contribute positively to or may damage the economic welfare of society.

A broad distinction may be drawn between two different sorts of growth strategy. First, media firms may expand 'horizontally' or within a single area of the activity, for example when one television broadcaster acquires another. Growth within a single sector of the media or a single business activity is sometimes referred to as 'monomedia' expansion. Monomedia expansion is a common strategy, allowing firms to expand their market share and, usually, to rationalize their resources and gain economies of scale. Second, 'cross-media' expansion involves expansion across two or more different sub-sectors of the media, for example when a newspaper publisher acquires radio broadcasting interests. Chapter 5 will investigate the economic gains associated with strategies of cross-media corporate growth. This chapter is concerned with the economic consequences of monomedia expansion.

This chapter and the next draw on the findings of recent empirical research into how and why exactly media firms benefit from expansion. This research was carried out in the late 1990s and focused on the economic and financial effects of corporate changes at a number of leading UK media organizations. The study involved an analysis of the profits performance and of the managerial experiences of several media firms engaged in varied corporate strategies. The aim was to find out to what extent the economic performance of these firms would support the general case in favour of liberalizing media and cross-media ownership rules. The evidence uncovered provides a good deal of useful information about the relationship between, on the one hand, the size and structure of media organizations and, on the other, their economic or financial efficiency.

Figure 4.1 indicates the firms that were included in the study and their media activities in the UK in 1997. The sample was selected purposively in order to assess a range of different corporate configurations, especially those that are affected by media ownership restrictions. Consequently, commercial broadcasting and national newspaper publishing activities are well represented within the group. Following on from when the study was completed in 1997, some additional corporate activity has taken place which, in one or two cases, has altered the size and general configuration of the firms under scrutiny.[1]

The study used qualitative and quantitative research methods but, as implied by the relatively small size of the chosen sample, a very heavy emphasis was placed on techniques of in-depth qualitative evidence gathering. In addition to analysing historic financial data and relevant industry estimates for each company, interviews were carried out with a range of senior and highly experienced managers across the sample group.[2] This resulted in a substantive body of findings concerning the relationship between the corporate configuration and the performance of these leading UK media firms.

| | TV b'Casting | TV prod. | National papers | Regional papers | Magazines | Radio b'Casting |
|---|---|---|---|---|---|---|
| EMAP plc | | | | √ | √ | √ |
| Grampian Television plc | √ | √ | | | | √ |
| Granada Media Group | √ | √ | | | | |
| Guardian Media Group | √ | √ | √ | √ | | |
| Mirror Group Newspapers plc | | | √ | √ | | |
| News International plc | √ | | √ | | | |
| Pearson plc | | √ | √ | √ | √ | |
| Scottish Television plc | √ | √ | | √ | | |
| United News & Media plc | √ | √ | √ | √ | | |

FIGURE 4.1   Activities of UK sample group in 1996–7

One main problem with investigating the association between a firm's size or its corporate shape and how well it is performing is that of deciding how to assess 'performance'. Economic performance is a 'multidimensional' concept (Wirth and Bloch, 1995). In any organization, different constituencies – for example, shareholders, senior management, employees or customers ('the public') – may have different ideas about what the organization's goals are, or should be. This is particularly true of the media sector where, as with other industries involved in cultural provision, some constituencies may regard social and cultural criteria as uppermost in judgements about performance and output.

Operating profitability – which is considered here – provides a workable focus for a comparative, quantitative analysis. Operating profit margins provide a measure of the level of profitability of a firm expressed in terms of its operating turnover and this is one of the most widely recognized accounting measures of performance. But, in the context of a cultural industry, profitability offers only a limited and narrow approach to the measurement of economic performance. Levels of operating profitability reveal little, for example, about the extent to which media firms are producing the ideal quantity, quality and mix of output to maximize societal welfare. On the other hand, profitability is a crucial determinant of the level of resources that will be attracted into the industry and made available for media provision, with accompanying welfare implications.

The quantitative data considered below is very heavily supplemented by qualitative evidence. The integration of interview findings provides a valuable means of breaking down and interpreting the economic welfare implications associated with different experiences of profit attainment at each of the sample firms. The use of qualitative evidence enables some interesting distinctions to be drawn between scale advantages mainly favouring the private interests of the firm (e.g. the ability of large media firms to exploit a dominant market position) and those which represent a benefit for the economy and society at large (e.g. the ability of large firms to use resources more cost-effectively).

The rest of this chapter is devoted to examining evidence concerning the economic implications of horizontal or 'monomedia' expansion. The performance of the sample group is analysed within a range of different media activities – television broadcasting, television production, radio broadcasting and newspaper publishing. As each sector is considered, the aim is to uncover what sort of relationship exists between the size or scale of operations of individual firms and their economic performance. Are larger players more profitable than smaller ones and, if so, why? What sort of efficiency gains or other scale advantages do media firms gain as they expand horizontally? By unravelling these questions, it becomes possible to assess the economic consequences of policies that either restrict or liberalize monomedia ownership.

## Television broadcasting

Five of the nine firms in this sample of UK firms were engaged in television broadcasting to a significant extent in 1996. Four were in control of regional terrestrial 'ITV' licences: Grampian, Granada, Scottish TV and United News & Media (UN&M). In addition to these four ITV companies, News International (NI) was involved in television broadcasting through its majority shareholding in BSkyB, the dominant direct-to-home satellite broadcaster in the UK.

With a collective peak-time viewing share of 37 per cent, ITV is by far the most popular commercial channel in Britain and comprises a network of 14 regional licences covering the whole of the UK (Competition Commission, 2000: 89). Ownership of these licences has been consolidating since the early 1990s and most are now controlled by just three firms: Granada Media, Carlton Communications and Scottish Media Group. The ITV network shares programmes through a system where each of the 14 licensees contributes a payment into a collective budget for the ITV schedule of programmes and, in return, receives the right to broadcast that schedule (interspersed with some dedicated local output) in their own region. Each licensee makes money by selling advertising slots in and around transmissions of the ITV network schedule in their own regions. Payments into the collective programme budget vary according to the respective revenue shares of participant in the network. So, ITV's arrangements for sharing costs involve some cross-subsidization of smaller regional licensees by larger ones. Even so, each participant – whether large or small – benefits from being able to transmit a much more expensive schedule of programmes than it could afford if it were trying to operate independently.

Plotting the operating profit margins of the five television broadcasters in the UK sample group against their share of the UK television market (as represented by share of the total television audiences) in 1996, a positive and fairly strong correlation emerges between size and performance. The largest player in the sample group – Granada – was by far the most profitable whereas its smallest rivals – Grampian and Scottish Television – achieved the lowest television operating margins. This relationship between market share and profits appears to hold true across different delivery platforms, both terrestrial and satellite (see Figure 4.2).

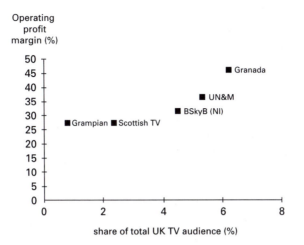

FIGURE 4.2: Market share and operating profit margins in TV broadcasting, 1996

The positive correlation between UK television broadcasters' market share and profitability is not entirely surprising. As has been noted by many previous writers, the broadcasting industry is strongly characterized by economies of scale. Extensive product-specific economies of scale exist in broadcasting because, once a delivery infrastructure is in place, the marginal costs of providing the service to an additional viewer (within one's transmission area or 'footprint') are zero or extremely low (Cave, 1989: 11–12). The overhead costs associated with providing a given service tend to be equal, regardless of audience size. So, all other things being equal, economies of scale will arise as larger audiences are translated into more revenue.

The experience of this UK sample group provides clear evidence that large broadcasters who are better placed to exploit economies of scale than small ones are likely to be more profitable. As one ITV chief executive explained:

> [In ITV] There are zero marginal costs with everything except networked programmes . . . There is no reason why, say, Granada's regional output or other costs should be any more expensive than STV's. They have exactly the same fixed costs . . . But Granada gets twice as much advertising revenue as STV.

Another ITV executive confirmed that the majority of costs associated with operating an ITV regional broadcasting service (e.g. local programme costs, administration and finance) must be borne, at more or less equal expense, by each individual licensee. But broadcasters with larger transmission areas can spread these costs across more viewers. So, in spite of the role played by the ITV network in helping to share peak-time programming costs, broadcasters with a large market share are inherently much more profitable than those with smaller market shares: 'For instance, there is a definite cost advantage to larger players on local programme costs. These are the same whatever the audience size . . .'

Of course, the relationship between the size or market share of television broadcasters and their profits performance may be subject to a range of additional complexities. In the UK, for example, different delivery systems for television have different cost and revenue structures, partly reflecting technology but also because of uneven regulation. The costs of operating a terrestrial service in the UK are generally higher than for cable or satellite because terrestrial services are subject to more expensive obligations *vis-à-vis* their programming output but, on the other hand, terrestrial services benefit from virtually universal access to UK viewers whereas cable and satellite were receivable in only some 25 per cent of UK homes in 1996.

Despite such important issues as differing technical transmission costs, expenses associated with fulfilling licence obligations and, indeed, variations in levels of managerial competence, the availability of economies of scale appears to be the single most influential factor governing the profitability of individual television broadcasters. And the opportunity to reduce per-viewer average costs, as audiences expand, will create a natural incentive for broadcasters to try to expand their market share.

Findings gathered from interviews carried out with managers across the UK sample of television companies confirm that broadcasting is characterized not only by economies of scale but also by 'economies of scope'. As with economies of scale, economies of scope are about cost savings and efficiency gains that are achieved as more of the broadcaster's output is consumed. In this case, however, savings are created by offering variations in the character or scope of the firm's output. Economies of scope – economies achieved through 'multi-product' production – are a fairly widespread feature amongst media enterprises and, again, they owe their existence to the public-good nature of media output. Economies of scope are generally defined as the economies available to firms 'large enough to engage efficiently in multi-product production and associated large scale distribution, advertising and purchasing' (Lipsey and Chrystal, 1995: 880). They arise when there are some shared overheads, or other efficiency gains available that make it more cost-effective for two or more related products to be produced and sold jointly, rather than separately. Savings may arise, for example, if specialist inputs gathered for one product can be re-used in another.

Economies of scope are common within the media because the nature of media output is such that it is possible for a product created for one audience or one market to be reformatted and sold to another. For example, an interview with a politician which is recorded for broadcast within a documentary might also be edited for inclusion within other news programmes, either on television or, indeed, on radio. The same television content can be repackaged into more than one television programme or more than one television service. The reformatting of broadcast output intended for one audience into another 'new' product suitable for a different audience creates economies of scope.

For television broadcasters who operate more than one service, economies of scope and of scale co-exist and the more homogeneity possible between all services, the greater the economies of scope. For example, to whatever extent the owner of two regional ITV licences, or two local cable licences, is able to share programming, or common elements within programming, a cost advantage can be achieved. In addition, as broadcasters expand the number of services within their control, opportunities arise to combine back-office activities (e.g. finance and administration) and specialist support functions (e.g. airtime sales and secondary programme sales).

The economies which arise from monomedia expansion in the UK television industry are summarized by one ITV chief executive in the following terms:

> The main costs that can be cut out in a merger situation within ITV are central services departments. These can be expensive: finance, IT, personnel, public affairs and head office administration. Also, transmission; everyone has their own transmission suites ... [Another area is] streamlining of programming, *if* that can be achieved – but the ITC polices licences pretty strongly. Benefits of this sort might be possible if the regions involved are contiguous [/overlapping] ...

Even where different television services are separately owned, collective economies might well be gained through broadcasters engaging in co-operative rather than competitive behaviour, for example sharing components of a programme service or sharing support functions. The formation of networks, such as the ITV network, is an obvious example of how co-operation between different owners can be exercised to secure collective benefits including, especially, economies of scale on programming costs. All 'partners' in the ITV network benefit from being able to share costs and negotiate as a collective entity.

On the other hand, rivalry between these different owners about the terms under which collective economies are shared out can sometimes act as an impediment to co-operation. An example of this is provided by ITV's 'in-house' transmission activities which, if centralized, would provide cost savings to all regional licensees in the network. Yet the opportunity to remove unnecessary replication of transmission resources throughout the ITV regions has not been seized. As one ITV Finance Director explains: 'Everyone [in ITV] is saying "Can't we have one transmission centre and can't it be mine?" It's the classic ITV situation where everyone can see that basically it's a good idea but nobody wants someone else to win so everybody ends up losing . . .' The efficiency gains forgone by such rivalry can be recovered only under circumstances of collective ownership. However, this is by no means the only incentive for broadcasters to expand their activities and consolidate their share of the market. As television broadcasters gain access to increasingly large audiences, they benefit not only from a reduction in average (per-viewer) costs, but also from revenue advantages associated with their increased 'critical mass'.

The way in which commercial airtime is sold to advertisers varies from one territory to another and, sometimes, between different broadcasters. Generally speaking, it is traded according to the size of the audience it reaches but sometimes it may be sold on a 'flat rate' basis – i.e. at a fixed price per (say, 30-second) advertising spot. When television advertising is sold according to the size of the audience, this typically involves looking at ratings predictions for the broadcaster's programme schedule and then booking sufficient slots to reach an audience of a given size and demographic profile on a cost-per-thousand (CPT) viewers basis.

According to evidence provided by executives from across the UK television sample group, advertising rates generally reflect the location and demographic profile of the audience that a television broadcaster is selling access to but, crucially, they are also influenced by the market power of the seller. Broadcasters with a large audience share or market share are able to command a premium in the CPT rates that they charge advertisers (Competition Commission, 2000: 198–204). Increased negotiating leverage with advertisers has been an important motive behind the consolidation of airtime sales activities within ITV in recent years. Whereas increased market power and increased negotiating leverage in the market for airtime sales may well benefit the profits of individual broadcasters, it is open to question whether this constitutes a general benefit for the market performance of the television sector as a whole.

## Television programme production

Television programme production is another sector of the industry where advantages of scale are in evidence. The output of television production companies – programmes – have public-good properties in the sense that, like whole broadcast services, one person's enjoyment of it does not exclude anyone else from also consuming it. No matter how many times a television programme is watched by viewers it still remains available to all. So, increasing marginal returns will be enjoyed as more and more customers for a television programme are added. The wider the audience for a programme, the more profitable it will become and the greater the economies of scale.

In the UK however, such economies tend to be enjoyed not by production companies themselves but by broadcasters. This is because the terms on which production companies supply programmes to broadcasters generally involve the at least partial assignation of secondary as well as primary transmission rights to the purchaser in return for a fixed production fee. In the UK, the powerful position occupied by dominant broadcasters has contributed to a situation where few independent programme producers share in any of the benefits associated with the 'public good' attributes of their output.

The pattern of apportionment of risks and of copyright ownership between producers and broadcasters has important implications for the financial well-being of production companies. In the US, the system of 'deficit financing' whereby broadcasters systematically pay a fee which is below production costs means that producers are obliged to take a share in the financial risks associated with developing new programmes. At the same time, US producers retain ownership of all rights associated with their own catalogues of programming output. By contrast, the 'cost-plus' system which prevails in the UK means that broadcasters usually cover all production costs and pay the producer a small fee or 'profit' but, in return, producers are expected to relinquish the majority of primary, secondary and other ancillary rights associated with their programmes.

So, in the UK, the predominant position of broadcasters in the supply chain means that few content producers are able to reap the benefits associated with low replication and marginal supply costs. 'Important' programme-makers may, however, acquire bargaining power and a competitive advantage over rivals in terms of their ability to gain orders for new shows and to negotiate some share in the incremental returns for a hit show. Size (market share) and 'importance' (reputation for supplying 'hit' programmes) are separate concepts but, in reality, a successful reputation and a busy production slate tend to be causally connected and mutually self-perpetuating.

Six companies in the UK sample group have significant television programme-making activities. Four of these are also active in television broadcasting, as indicated in Figure 4.1 above. The remaining two –

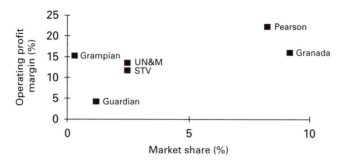

FIGURE 4.3   Market share and operating profit margins in TV production, 1996

Guardian Media Group and Pearson – are the owners of 'independent' production companies.[3]

Plotting the estimated operating profit margins against the market shares of these six companies in 1996 (Figure 4.3), we see some evidence of a general relationship between these variables, in that the two largest companies – Granada and Pearson – achieve the best margins. The exception to a generally strong correlation between size and performance is Grampian Television which, with only 0.3 per cent of the market, nevertheless achieved above-average margins on its production activities in 1996. The explanation for this may reside in the fact that, to a much greater extent than any of the other broadcaster-producers above, Grampian's production activity comprises servicing its *own* broadcasting operation.[4] Excluding Grampian, the evidence of a link between size and performance is a good deal stronger.[5] Clearly, however, qualitative evidence is needed to provide a fuller account of how scale affects the performance of television production companies.

Interview findings gathered from this sample of UK television programme-makers generally confirm that advantages of one kind or another will accrue to large scale television producers. On the other hand, it is widely agreed that programme production tends to be a 'buyer's market' (i.e. that the supply of production capability exceeds orders available from broadcasters) so that the key to success for a programme-maker is not so much size as the ability to create hit programmes. On closer inspection, it becomes apparent that these two issues (size and ability to create hits) are not entirely dissociated. As one executive explains:

> As an 'independent' it is very difficult to get into the primetime slot – unless you have a great show – and the only way you can establish a great show is by having it on, so it's a bit of a vicious circle. What being big does for you is it allows you to get a new show on air . . . it gives you negotiating

leverage (you can say, I won't raise the price of X if you take Y). That is the principal 'economy' or scale advantage.

The advantages of greater scale (or status as a supplier) are not only to do with spreading risk and accumulating negotiating power but are also, at least to some extent, to do with economies of scale in production in the more traditional sense. Large scale production will not necessarily bring about a reduction in input costs through bulk discounts because, in television, 'talent' or individual artists tend to comprise the main raw material. On the other hand, overhead costs can be spread, at a reducing marginal rate, over increasing output levels. The Finance Director of a major UK television production enterprise explains the benefits of an expansion in activities as follows:

> You need a certain infrastructure regardless of size: finance (to do costs and budgets); legal affairs (to do contracts). [As production expands] you will get a certain level of economies of scale on these, on Errors & Omissions insurance, and marginal savings on casting . . . If you've got the studios, staff and facilities in place, you can get better use out of them.
>
> But the problem is that programmes are all individual pieces . . . You can't assume that if you make a few more programmes cheaply . . . [a broadcaster] will want them. Also, a lot is 'talent' based. You might, for example, want to do twenty episodes of *Prime Suspects* in a year, but the main star might not want to . . . 'Talent' is not susceptible to the economies of scale argument.

Production companies with a busier production slate are evidently able to achieve economies of scale through improved rates of overhead recovery. However, demand is relatively unpredictable, which makes it difficult to sustain a consistently optimal rate of output. Also, whether an expansion in output will bring additional economies of scale depends on the nature of the programme. In general, because of high initial development costs, the cost of assembling sets, contracting 'talent' etc., the production of a 'one-off' programme will tend to be more expensive than producing a series. Similarly, as one independent producer suggests, recommissions of a second or third series of the same programme tend to yield economies of scale:

> The major development costs you write off in the first run – the cost of developing the format is put into the first six shows because you don't know if you will get a second series commissioned. Therefore, any subsequent series is more profitable . . .

But the level of scale economies available on production costs for long-running series is dependent on the terms of access between the producer and whatever ingredient lends the programme its special audience appeal.

'Human asset specificity' and the prevalence of short-term contracts and freelancing makes it difficult for television production companies to avoid transaction costs (Moschandreas, 1994: 65, 68). If the success of a programme is dependent on specific writers, actors, presenters or directors then, subject to the terms of their contracts, these individuals may effectively be able to halt production of a further series (by withdrawal of their labour) or else to inflate production costs by renegotiating their remuneration.

So, although the production of a long-running series should theoretically lead to economies of scale (through, for example, improved efficiency as the production team becomes more experienced at working together), the extent of those economies in practice will depend on the nature of the programme (whether, for example, it is studio based or requires many expensive changes of location) and – in particular – the programme-maker's ability to constrain the price of programme inputs for which there are no perceived substitutes. Some programmes have few such vital ingredients and are good 'bankers', whereas with others success may immediately be accompanied by inflationary pressure on costs.

More generally, companies with a large scale of production activity stand to benefit from greater expertise and lower per-unit overhead costs across a range of support functions that are integral to the business, such as finance and legal affairs. Sales of secondary transmission rights is another vital function and, while this may be subcontracted to a specialist third party (such as an international programme distributor), there are clear benefits for companies with a large critical mass in production. A bigger production slate creates a brand image and reputation which can be exploited in domestic secondary and international programme markets and it also creates economies within the marketing and selling functions. As one large independent producer explains:

> If you're going to distribute programmes in, say, Australia or France or Los Angeles, you need more than one show to justify the fixed costs of having a sales office there! A big catalogue makes secondary markets more accessible and more economical to exploit.

## Radio broadcasting

The economics of radio broadcasting is very similar to that of television. Only two of the companies in the sample group have been directly involved in radio broadcasting although others (e.g. Guardian Media Group) have extensive interests in the sector though minority shareholdings in one or several radio stations. EMAP, through its ownership of 17 commercial radio stations in 1996, had developed into one of the largest radio broadcasters in the UK. By examining the experience of EMAP as it has built up its presence in radio broadcasting over recent years (mainly through acquisitions), it is possible to trace a linear relationship between its market share and the levels of operating profitability it has achieved (Figure 4.4).

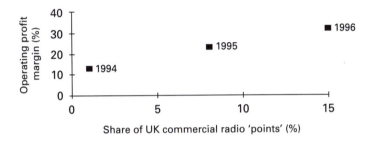

FIGURE 4.4    Market share and operating margins: EMAP Radio Division, 1994–96

The presence of such a correlation is not entirely surprising given that, as with the television industry, marginal transmission costs are low or zero, thus creating natural economies of scale for radio broadcasters. In much the same way as with television, however, the practical extent to which economies can be exploited by an individual radio broadcaster is not solely dependent on total audience share. Since UK radio licences are limited by fixed transmission areas, a crucial factor is the *composition* of that market share in terms of the number of distinct services (or sets of operating costs) it represents. Setting aside the issue of cost differentials for alternative types of radio content, it seems clear that, for any given level of total audience share, a broadcaster that only has to provide a single radio service can naturally avail itself of more economies of scale (lower per-listener costs) than one providing several different services.

Thus, the availability of scale economies for a radio broadcaster is dependent on the number of licensed services being provided, and how 'different' they are, as well as total audience share. Where there is little overlap between the transmission areas associated with each licence, an opportunity may exist to share a common service (or elements thereof) across a network of radio stations held in common ownership. Because the majority of commercial radio broadcasting licences in the UK serve relatively small local transmission areas, economies of scope are a feature even more prevalent in the radio than in the television industry.

## Newspaper publishing

Looking at size against operating profit performance for those companies in the sample group involved in publishing national newspapers, it once again emerges that the largest players – News International (NI) and Mirror Group (MGN) – achieve an operating profit performance which is superior to that of their smaller competitors (see Figure 4.5). However, when interpreting the comparative performance of this particular set of 'rivals', special circumstances surrounding the smallest national newspaper publishers in the sample group must be taken into account.

The Guardian Media Group's negative operating performance reflects the fact that its national newspaper division is not run to conventional profit-maximizing objectives. The Guardian Media Group, unlike all eight other firms in the sample, is not listed on the Stock Exchange but is wholly owned by a private trust (the Scott Trust), one of whose primary objectives is to ensure the continuation of its 'liberal' national newspaper title, the *Guardian*, irrespective of whether or not the newspaper is operating profitably (Schlesinger, 1994: 16). In addition, the company with the smallest share of national circulation – Pearson – occupies a unique market position since its only title is a specialist publication with a unique set of cost and revenue variables. The niche position occupied by the *Financial Times* helps to explain why Pearson achieves a better operating margin than either of its two larger rivals – United News & Media and Guardian Media Group. Not surprisingly then, the correlation between size and performance for the sample group is considerably stronger when Pearson and the Guardian are left out than when they are included.[6]

However, the value of quantitative analysis for such a small sample group is clearly very limited and, as before, information collected through interviews provides a valuable means of examining more closely how exactly market share affects profitability in the UK newspaper publishing sector.

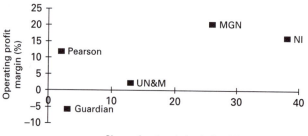

FIGURE 4.5  Market share and operating profit margins for national newspaper groups, 1996

While control over a large market share creates the *potential* to exploit a range of economies of scale, it does not necessarily follow that, in practice, companies with control over large circulation shares will achieve higher operating margins than companies with a low share of circulation, as the Chief Executive of one newspaper group explains:

> Yes, there *are* economies of scale but [on the other hand] you can have a unique market position, for example, a monopoly franchise [in a certain area] . . . Volume isn't necessarily the only thing that counts and having groups of newspapers clumped together isn't necessarily the only thing that counts – but it *is* helpful . . . [when] you *do* have more than one title under the same infrastructure.

Because the marginal costs involved in selling one additional copy of the same edition of a newspaper are relatively low, publishers tend to benefit from product-specific economies of scale as circulations expand. Marginal costs are positive since (unlike broadcasting) the product is delivered in a tangible form, involving printing and distribution costs. However, according to the evidence supplied by this sample group of UK newspaper publishers, editorial overheads tend to be the largest single component of expenditure and these do not necessarily change as consumption of the product expands or contracts. The editorial overheads associated with publishing any given title tend to be fixed, regardless of actual circulation volume and so, all other things being equal, economies of scale arise as larger levels of readership are translated into more revenue.

All of the newspaper publishers in the UK sample group suggest that economies of scope as well as scale co-exist for newspaper owners publishing more than one title. Publishers of several titles may be able to combine and rationalize back-office activities such as administration, finance and personnel. Economies of scope may arise because of the opportunity to negotiate better collective terms on input prices (e.g. paper) or support services (e.g. printing or distribution). Specialist functions such as advertising sales may be shared across several titles, thus reducing costs. However, when it comes to the editorial process itself, there is disagreement in the views expressed by different publishers about the extent to which economies of scope can be gained. The perspectives offered by this UK sample group indicate an interesting disagreement as to how far the process of sharing costs between different newspaper titles can go.

At one extreme, some senior managers in the UK newspaper industry suggest that the most cost-effective way to produce a given range of titles is to draw, as appropriate to each title's individual character, on what is regarded as a completely flexible internal pool of shared journalistic expertise. The Chief Executive of one newspaper group explained his approach thus:

> [Title X] . . . has a whole machinery for covering television soap operas and the Royal Family, so why would it be duplicated by . . . [Title Y]?
>
> Why doesn't . . . [Title Y] simply *leverage* the resource brought in by its partner newspaper, and customize it, so that it's all in the editing process rather than the gathering process?

However, many are sceptical about the benefits available from trying to integrate as many cost functions as possible for competing titles. Combining the journalistic functions of different titles may yield cost savings but a majority of UK publishers seem to feel that this would jeopardize the individual tone of each product. According to one Finance Director:

> We've looked at all this and it is not any easy one . . . Sharing journalists across different titles would be extreme. It is *very* hard to do . . . You risk losing the independence of your title.

Even where newspaper titles are separately owned, collective economies can be and, to some extent are, exploited in the UK national newspaper industry by sharing or contracting out to a third party activities such as printing and distribution. But rivalry between newspaper owners inevitably serves to constrain the extent of such cost-sharing so that, as with the UK broadcasting sectors, consolidated ownership remains the key to certain cost reductions.

In addition, qualitative evidence from the sample group indicates that UK newspaper owners with a large market share may acquire advantages through exercising their 'market power'. Dominant newspaper publishers clearly have greater resources with which to engage in or withstand aggressive competitive pricing strategies. Also, as elsewhere in the media, newspaper advertising rates (per reader) are influenced to some extent by the bargaining power or 'critical mass' of the seller. To the extent that the exercise of market power by large newspaper groups may serve to impede competition – for example, through predatory pricing techniques – this advantage for the individual firm translates into an obstacle for market efficiency and a disadvantage for consumers. Hence, strategic benefits of scale for the firm cannot, unambiguously, be regarded as positive 'economic' gains in the same way as improved cost-efficiency through a better use of resources would be (Martin, 1993: 313–17).

## Monomedia expansion and economic performance

The general weight of this evidence derived from the experiences of leading participants in the UK media industry suggests a strong and positive correlation between monomedia firm size and profitability. Strategies of monomedia expansion are likely to result in increased operating profit margins for television companies, radio broadcasters and newspaper publishers. The higher profitability achieved by bigger media firms is largely (although not entirely) accounted for by efficiency gains such as increased opportunities to reap economies of scale and scope and to rationalize resources. Qualitative evidence firmly indicates that, although many factors other than size can and do affect the performance of individual media firms, a causal link *is* present between the market share and the, at least *potential*, economic performance of firms operating in the television, radio and newspaper sectors in the UK.

Although the relationship between size and profits performance is generally positive for each of the four sub-sectors of the media considered above, it is not always a perfectly linear one. For example, the correlation coefficient for the television broadcasting and national newspaper sectors may be calculated as 0.876 and 0.663 respectively. Clearly, then, some factors other than market share also have a bearing on the performance of individual media organizations. According to the qualitative evidence provided by most interviewees in this sample group, those variables other than size which are likely to have the greatest bearing on the performance of individual media companies are variations in managerial efficiency or niche product positions.

Nevertheless, an association between market share and profits is evident within television and radio broadcasting and within newspaper publishing. The existence of a link between the profitability and market share (or positions of dominance) of individual firms confirms the general conclusions offered by industrial economics theory (George et al., 1992: 302). But evidence gathered from across this sample of leading UK media firms has helped to clarify the precise nature and causes of this link in the context of media industries.

Economies of scale have been identified as a crucial factor in all the main sectors of activity. In television broadcasting, the marginal cost of transmitting to an extra television viewer is usually negligible, although this depends on the distribution system concerned. With terrestrial television transmitted over the airwaves, the marginal cost is typically zero, unless a new transmitter has to be built to reach that extra viewer. With cable television, the connection cost has to be included. For pay television services, some marginal subscriber management costs will arise, but these are relatively modest. Generally speaking, it costs virtually nothing to supply a television or radio broadcast service to an extra customer, so there are great economies of scale involved as the audience grows.

In newspaper publishing, the marginal costs involved in selling one additional copy of the same edition of a newspaper are relatively low, so product-specific economies of scale will arise as circulations expand. The evidence provided by UK newspaper publishers shows that editorial and administrative overheads represent major costs that are relatively fixed or are not directly influenced by fluctuations in circulation levels. So, although marginal costs (of, for example, distribution and printing) are present in newspaper publishing, it is nonetheless a sector that is strongly characterized by economies of scale.

The widespread availability of economies of scale in the media industry is generally associated with low replication costs for media output. Initial production costs (i.e. the cost of creating the first or master copy) may be high but then very few marginal costs are incurred as the product is replicated and distributed or sold over and over again to ever-greater numbers of consumers. However, even within the expensive initial content production phase, economies of scale may be present. The experience of those UK media companies engaged in content production suggests that, as output expands, marginal costs (say, the cost of creating one additional hour of a television drama) may well be lower than average costs (total production costs divided by the number of hours of drama already produced).

The experience of a number of UK companies involved in television production indicates that, as the level or volume of production activity increases, the firm may derive economies of scale on fixed overheads by, for example, making better use of capital equipment (cameras, post-production facilities, etc.) or salaried personnel. So, expansion may be motivated by the desire to increase the use of under-utilized resources. According to the evidence, production companies that expand horizontally and increase their output may also enjoy productivity gains because of the opportunity for specialization of tasks as the firm grows larger. The realization of scale economies may, arguably, facilitate higher levels of gross investment and speedier adoption of new technologies.

There is also strong empirical evidence that economies of scope – savings that arise as the firm diversifies its output – are prevalent in each of the main sub-sectors of the media. As a broadcaster or newspaper publisher expands and increases the number of products or services it is delivering, the experience of UK media players suggests that valuable opportunities will arise to combine specialist functions such as advertising sales and back-office activities such as finance and administration. If the same media content or intellectual property can be exploited across more than one product or service, further economies of scope will be gained. The opportunity to share the use of specialized resources and expertise across more than one media product is a key incentive for firms to engage in strategies of horizontal expansion.

So, economies of scope help to explain widespread tendencies towards monomedia expansion and the high number of 'multi-product' firms. For example, EMAP plc currently owns some 19 separate local radio stations throughout the UK. News Corporation owns four major national newspaper titles. The presence of both economies of scale and scope in the media implies a natural gravitation towards oligopoly market structures and towards large scale multi-product firms. Provided that product quality does not suffer through sharing or spreading costs amongst more consumers or over a greater number of media products, then strategies of monomedia expansion will yield efficiency gains which, in theory, ought to benefit societal welfare. However, if cost-savings are achieved at the expense of viewers' or readers' utility then it cannot be said that expansion leads to improved efficiency.

But leaving aside efficiency gains, another important advantage associated with having a large market presence in any sector of the media (or of cross-owning media products in several sectors) is that it gives the firm greater 'critical mass'. Firms with a large market share have greater negotiating leverage in deals with suppliers and with buyers: so large newspaper publishers in the UK tend to get a better deal on paper and newsprint prices than smaller ones. A dominant firm also has greater ability to exercise some control over the prices it charges its customers. The largest players in the UK television, radio and newspaper sectors are all able to charge premium prices for their advertising when compared (on a CPT basis) with smaller firms.

The greater 'market power' which large UK media firms command undoubtedly serves to enhance their profitability. This is all well and good for the firms in question, but it also has the potential to harm consumer interests and to threaten the efficient operation of media markets. If dominant players are able to charge too much for advertising then this may adversely affect competition and excessive costs may be passed on to consumers through higher product prices. To the extent that the exercise of market power by large media groups serves to impede competition then the strategic advantage it confers upon the individual firm simultaneously acts as an obstacle to market efficiency and represents a disadvantage for consumers.

On the basis of the evidence considered here, arguments in favour of high monomedia ownership ceilings, when based on economic efficiency criteria, appear to be generally well founded. Strategies of monomedia expansion not only increase the profitability of individual media firms but can potentially deliver a range of valuable efficiency gains that contribute positively to economic welfare. But, as with any other sector of economic activity, horizontal expansion strategies in the media pose a threat when individual firms are allowed to acquire excessive market power. So, a strong economic case can be argued in favour of encouraging media firms to expand until all available cost-efficiencies and economies are being maximized, but a countervailing economic argument exists in favour of sustaining competition at levels sufficient to prevent abuses of market power.

---

## Notes

1. Scottish Television plc (now 'Scottish Media Group plc') acquired Grampian Television plc in the summer of 1997. In addition, Granada Group plc took over Yorkshire-Tyne Tees Television in 1998 and, in 2000, Granada acquired the Anglia and Meridian ITV licences from United News & Media plc.

2. The Annual Report and Accounts of each company provided the main source of financial data. Calculations of market share by sector are based on relevant UK audience and readership figures published by the Independent Television Commission (ITC), the Radio Authority (RA) and the Audience Bureau of Circulations (ABC).

3. The 1990 Broadcasting Act defined an 'independent' production company as one which is not more than 15 per cent owned by a TV broadcasting company and which itself, owns no more than 15 per cent of a TV broadcaster. The 1995 (Independent Productions) Broadcasting Order amended the threshold for cross-ownership between 'independent' producers and broadcasters, raising it from 15 per cent to 25 per cent.

4. Most vertically integrated ITV companies account separately for, on the one hand, externally commissioned programme production work (e.g. for the ITV network) and, on the other, 'in-house' production (i.e. production which directly services their broadcasting operations); the former is generally recognized as a distinct profit centre whereas the latter is treated as a 'cost of sale' within the broadcasting division. Since, in reality, 'in-house' (e.g. regional) productions are transferred at cost from the production to the broadcasting division, the operating margins ascribed to such activity are largely *notional* and may vary widely, depending on the accounting conventions deployed (e.g. whether the use of facilities is charged at a full market rate or a marginal cost rate).

5. The value of the correlation coefficient for the entire six companies in the television production sample in 1996 is 0.634, indicating a relatively modest

positive association between the variables. Recalculation of the correlation excluding Grampian yields a value of 0.802, indicating a much stronger relationship. The correlation coefficient is a mathematical measure of the strength of the relationship between two variables, calculated on the basis of the average standard deviation between these variables. Its value always falls somewhere between −1 and +1 and, the further the value is away from zero, the stronger the correlation between the two variables.

6. The correlation coefficient for the entire sample is 0.663 but rises to 0.747 when Pearson and the Guardian Media Group are left out

# 5

# Cross-Media Expansion

The activities of media firms need not be confined to a single sub-sector of the industry; frequently they span several of these. The development of 'empires' that spread across newspaper and magazine publishing, books and films or television and the Internet is a widespread phenomenon evident in virtually all developed media economies. The ongoing globalization of media markets and convergence in technology between different sectors of the media and between media and other industries have caused many media firms to adapt their business and corporate strategies accordingly. This chapter examines the economic implications of cross-media concentrations of ownership and sets out to uncover the economic gains associated with strategies of cross-media corporate growth.

Convergence and globalization appear to have encouraged trends towards concentrated cross-media ownership, with the growth of integrated conglomerates (Time Warner/AOL, Pearson, Bertelsmann etc.) whose activities span several areas of the industry. As discussed in Chapter 3, strategies of growth and diversification make sense, at least in theory. Highly concentrated firms who can spread production costs across wider product and geographic markets will, of course, benefit from natural economies of scale and scope in the media. Enlarged, diversified and vertically integrated groups seem well suited to exploit the technological and other market changes sweeping across the media and communications industries. These market changes, when combined with the public-good characteristics of media discussed above, provide what appears to be a compelling explanation for why profit-maximizing media firms should pursue strategies of empire-building. But there are alternative schools of thought on what it is that drives firms – media or otherwise – to expand. Other approaches suggest that expansion is usually more to do with satisfying the personal interests of managers than with maximizing profits.

Most firms these days take the form of a public limited company (plc) and are run by managers rather than by owners (shareholders). Ownership and control of the firm are therefore separate and, because managers have different objectives from shareholders, a divergence from profit maximization becomes possible. Managers are, of course, concerned with keeping up profits, but they also have their own personal concerns. Marris – an influential management theorist – suggested that a principal aim of managers is to try to expand the firms they are running, at all costs, and irrespective of whether this will make the firm more efficient or more profitable (Moschandreas, 1994: 284–5). The suggestion by Marris, Williamson and other managerial theorists is that growth of the firm is the main objective because this raises managerial utility 'by bringing higher salaries, power, status, and job security' (Griffiths and Wall, 1999: 91).

So one reason why managers try to expand the firm might be because salary levels for senior management are quite closely linked to the scale of a firm's activities. In the UK, for example, the Chief Executive of British Telecommunications earns more than the Chief Executive of Border Television. In addition, fast-growing rather than static firms will give higher remuneration to managers. As a firm grows, its senior managers become powerful captains of industry and are often invited to join prestigious industry bodies, such as the Confederation of British Industry (CBI). Being the senior manager of a large media firm is a powerful and politically influential role.

Another reason why managers try to build empires may be because it makes it more difficult for their firm to be taken over by a predator. Senior managers usually want to avoid takeover and the risk of replacement by a new management team. By expanding – e.g. through acquisition of several smaller companies – a firm makes itself a more expensive and difficult target for takeover. The less prone a firm is to takeover, the greater the job security for its senior managers.

Most scholars of industrial economics accept that managers have some element of discretion to pursue goals other than profit maximization and that managerial agendas can sometimes help explain corporate behaviour. On the other hand, deterministic approaches to expansion on the part of the firm tend to emphasize profit maximization as the fundamental motive. As far as the media industry is concerned, motives other than profit could well play some role in encouraging strategies of corporate growth. The remainder of this chapter draws on recent empirical research carried out in the UK to illustrate the sorts of benefit and advantage that accrue, in practice, as media firms expand.

At least two different sorts of cross-sectoral expansion in the media have been subject to regulatory interventions of one kind or another –

namely, 'diagonal' and 'vertical'. Vertical growth involves expanding either 'forward' into succeeding stages or 'backward' into preceding stages in the supply chain. Diagonal or 'lateral' expansion occurs when firms diversify into new business areas: a telecommunications operator may expand diagonally into television, or newspaper publishers may expand diagonally into television broadcasting, or radio companies may diversify into magazine publishing.

The experiences of the sample group of leading UK media firms allows both strategies to be examined. Evidence gathered from this group of firms concerning the implications of cross-sectoral expansion is analysed focusing on two possible combinations of cross-media ownership which, in the UK as in many other countries, have been subject to special regulatory interventions. The first is television broadcasting plus newspaper publishing – an example of diagonal cross-media ownership. The second combination is that of television broadcasting plus content production – an example of vertical cross-media ownership. As each such configuration is considered, the aim is to find out what sort of relationship exists between strategies of cross-ownership and economic performance. Are diversified players more profitable than media firms operating in one sector alone and, if so, why? What sort of efficiency gains or other scale advantages do media firms gain as they expand operations and diversify into related or alternative fields of activity?

## Diagonal growth

Diagonal growth refers to developing the business sideways or 'diagonally' into what may be perceived as complementary activities (e.g. newspapers plus magazines, or television plus radio). In theory, a variety of reasons may exist why firms operating in one industry or sub-sector of activity might move across into another. For example, the perceived availability of higher rates of return in a newly emerging sector of activity may draw entrants from more mature or from declining industries. Other economic incentives include the perceived availability, through combining new with existing operations, of either incremental revenue advantages or collective cost-efficiencies by the shared use of specialized resources or expertise.

According to evidence gathered from the UK sample group, many strategies of diagonal cross-media expansion result in positive synergies and gains. The combinations of cross-media ownership that yield the most significant economic efficiencies are those which facilitate sharing of common specialized content or of a common distribution infrastructure

– i.e. those which give rise to what Albarran and Dimmick have described as 'economies of multiformity' (1996: 41).

When a media firm's output is characterized by a particular theme or subject matter, then expanding operations into several different sectors will usually create important synergies. For example, Pearson's specialization in providing one particular form of media content – management information – enables it to exploit economies of scale and scope across several different products (e.g. the *Financial Times* newspaper, *FT* business magazines, *FT* newsletters, *FT* newscasts, etc.) and modes of delivery (e.g. print, broadcast).

A focus on one particular type of content may enable the firm to build very strong brands that are more likely to be successful in crossing over from one platform to another. So specialization and the development of recognizable brands (such as the *Financial Times*) make it easier for firms to exploit new vehicles for delivery of media content, such as the Internet. In addition, diversified media companies such as Pearson or EMAP are able to reduce costs by exploiting overlaps in the production process for some of their products. Cross-ownership between, for example, newspaper publishing, magazine publishing and book publishing creates potential economies in any processes and inputs that are common to all of these activities, such as printing and purchasing paper.

So, even where media products seem quite 'different' (e.g. radio and newspapers, or television and books), economies are theoretically available. However, according to the qualitative findings collected from the UK sample group, much will depend on how specialized the content of each product is and how readily such content can be repackaged into different formats – i.e. the relationship between the marginal costs of reformatting content and the marginal revenues likely to be raised through selling it again in additional product markets.

As far as cross-ownership within traditional sectors of the media is concerned, quantitative data for the UK sample group is quite limited but several firms within the group were in a good position to offer in-depth qualitative evidence concerning the economics of cross-ownership between television and newspapers – see Figure 4.1, p. 46. News International, Mirror Group, United News & Media and Scottish Television all had fairly significant interests both in newspapers and television broadcasting in the UK in the mid-late 1990s and some had embarked on cross-sectoral expansion only recently.

The range of perspectives offered by the UK sample group provides a rich and interesting body of qualitative evidence concerning the potential advantages of expansion from newspapers to television broadcasting, and vice versa. Findings suggest that, although there is plenty of scope for content-sharing between text-based products (e.g. electronic and print provision), this is not necessarily true of text-based plus audio products, or text-based plus audiovisual products. In fact, according to the views expressed by most senior UK media managers interviewed, there is little or no overlap between production techniques in the television and newspaper sectors, or between production techniques in the newspaper and radio sectors. Technological convergence of these sectors has *not* arrived. So although, for instance, news-gathering activities might be shared (especially where there is a common locality or some other specialisation), there is a limit to any available economies of scope between newspaper publishing and television broadcasting.

Across leading UK media companies, there is a strong tendency towards skepticism about whether television broadcasting and newspaper publishing offer any substantive synergies. Apart from Scottish TV, few shared the conviction that combined advertising packages bring potential benefit. At the same time, there was widespread agreement that the skills involved in newspaper production and distribution are different from those required in the television industry, and vice versa. The 'bi-media' approach introduced at the BBC in the 1990s may be feasible to some extent within broadcasting, but it does not extend to the combination of newspaper publishing with television broadcasting activities. Economies of scope are not seen as an incentive for cross-ownership of television and newspapers. Thus, the economic rationale for combining newspaper with television operations would appear to be quite limited. As one corporate strategist points out:

> There are actually a lot of successful groups who have operated both, always operating each distinctly – with the exception of, occasionally, slavishly cross-promoting [using one product (say, an established newspaper title) to promote another (say, a new television service)] . . . I do not think that television and newspapers are a 'natural' diversification from each other . . .

According to most managers in the sample group, the *only* special advantage of cross-owning television and newspapers appears to be the opportunity to cross-promote products. Some opportunities may arise to combine back-office activities or, perhaps, to introduce improvements in managerial efficiency but, apparently, no more so than would arise in any merger involving other (loosely related) sectors of activity.

If 'natural' economies of scope are non-existent and revenue advantages are generally difficult to achieve, it follows that few economic benefits can be directly or solely attributable to the fact of cross-ownership of television and newspapers. So why do such mergers take place? Again, qualitative findings provide some interesting revelations concerning the motivations which underlie cross-sectoral expansion between newspaper and television companies in the UK.

It is widely suggested that the main point of lobbying for a relaxation in UK cross-media ownership restrictions has been to clear the way for newspaper proprietors to expand beyond their own sector (where demand is in gradual long-term decline) into the more profitable growth areas in the media (i.e. terrestrial television). As one newspaper executive notes, this argument has no basis in terms of improved operational or economic efficiency but, instead, is based solely on securing a low-risk route to long-term earnings growth for incumbent newspaper proprietors and shareholders:

> [Our] . . . original argument for going from newspapers to television was that advertisers were moving to television from the press. We want to diversify risk; to manage the decline in this medium for advertising [newspapers] and take some of the upside in the new growth area. That is fine but it's actually an *investment* statement, not a management statement . . .
>
> Cross-media ownership synergies was very much the argument put forward [to the Government], but it is not what people were after, as is borne out by what is happening.

This differentiation between two motives – efficiency versus risk-spreading – is important and introduces the question of what is, and what is *not*, a legitimate concern for public policy.

The commercial incentive for a newspaper proprietor to move into television can be much more readily identified than the incentive for a television company to move into newspaper publishing. If opportunities to build incremental revenues are limited, and economies of scope are not an intrinsic feature, then it is difficult to see why profit-maximizing television companies should choose to expand in the direction of a low-growth area such as newspaper publishing.

One possible motivation highlighted by companies who have recently engaged in expansion is that greater synergies and 'economies of multi-formity' between newspaper publishing and television broadcasting may develop over the long term. For example, growth in electronic communications may create demand for new products based on both audiovisual images and text. As far as newly expanded television-newspaper companies are concerned, the perceived long-term potential for synergies to emerge, and increased flexibility to respond to such future opportunities, were important considerations behind their respective decisions to expand diagonally into each other's sectors. In other words, the dynamic of anticipated technological change may, in this case, have exerted a significant influence.

Such considerations are clearly valid on commercial grounds but, as another possibility, motives other than profit maximization – i.e. managerial motives – may also play a role in cross-sectoral mergers between television and newspapers. As discussed above, managerial theorists have frequently suggested that the desire by managers to 'build empires' is an important motivation for diagonal growth (Martin, 1993: 280) and, indeed, a number of interviewees amongst the sample group express the belief that the true explanation for UK television companies' expansion into newspaper publishing is as 'a defensive move' against hostile takeover, i.e. making the enlarged company less attractive to potential predators. Considerable regional sensitivities prevail about the possibility of losing control of media companies to 'outsiders' and this may encourage conglomerate expansion, notwithstanding any negative efficiency implications.

Other factors cited as encouraging such takeovers include 'the human factor' – the desire by managements simply to increase their own prestige by increasing the overall size of their firm – and the 'flying speed' argument: a growing company creates positive morale and is easier to manage than one that is contracting or standing still. Thus, takeovers between television and newspaper operators may have more to do with a convergence between the interests of the management of television companies (in not losing control of their operations) and the need for newspaper proprietors to sustain their long-term profit prospects, than with any distant prospect of technological convergence.

In summary, the qualitative evidence supplied by this UK sample group indicates that even though strategies of diagonal expansion across television and newspapers sometimes create worthwhile benefits for individual firms and their shareholders or managements, it does not follow that such expansion will give rise to any general economic gains. Since production and distribution techniques are different for broadcasting and newspapers, relatively few opportunities to make better use of collective resources will arise directly from diagonal cross-ownership of these particular sectors of the media.

### Vertical integration

The production of any good or service usually involves several stages which can be separated out and studied more closely. A 'vertical supply chain' may be used to represent an industry's activities broken down into a sequence which starts 'upstream' at the early stages in the production process, works its way through succeeding or 'downstream' stages where

FIGURE 5.1    The vertical supply chain for media

the product is processed and refined, and finishes up as it is supplied or sold to the customer. This provides a useful framework for analysing strategies of vertical cross-media expansion: see Figure 5.1.

For media industries, it is possible to identify a number of broad stages in the vertical supply chain which connects producers with consumers. These include, first, the business of creating media content (e.g. gathering news stories, or making television or radio programmes). Second, media content has to be assembled into a product, for example a newspaper or television service. Third, the finished product must be distributed or sold to consumers. All of these broad stages in the vertical supply chain for media are interdependent: media content has no value unless it is distributed to an audience, and distribution infrastructures and outlets are of little interest without content to disseminate. No single stage is more important than another: all are interrelated. So, the performance of every firm involved in the supply chain will be threatened if a bottleneck develops – i.e. if one player manages to monopolize any single stage in the chain: if one company gains control over all the substitute inputs at an upstream stage, or all of the facilities required for distribution, then rivals will be put at a considerable disadvantage and consumers are also likely to suffer.

The interdependent relation of different phases in the supply chain has important implications for what sort of corporate growth strategies media firms will choose to pursue. The desire for more control over the market environment may act as an incentive for firms to diversify into additional upstream or downstream phases. Vertical integration refers to the extent to which related activities up and down the supply chain are integrated or are carried out jointly by 'vertically integrated' firms whose activities span two or more stages in the supply process. Media firms may expand their operations vertically either by investing new resources or else by acquiring other firms that are already established in succeeding or preceding stages in the supply chain.

The activities of the television industry can be vertically disaggregated into several key stages. First, production of television programmes is carried out by programme-makers. Programmes are then sold to 'packagers' who assemble television schedules. Then, the assembled television service, as a package, is distributed onwards to viewers by broadcasters. Some service packagers are broadcasters themselves but others are separate intermediaries, such as the major US networks. The 'distribution' phase for broadcast television can sometimes be broken into more than one stage. For example, with pay-television, 'distribution' (carried out by broadcasters) may be separate from consumer interface (carried out by subscriber management services).

Some television companies are involved in all the major stages along the vertical supply chain. Amongst the UK sample group, four companies – Grampian, Granada, Scottish TV and United News & Media – had significant interests both in television broadcasting and in programme production activities in the UK in 1996–97. Two others – Guardian Media Group and Pearson – were the owners of 'independent' production companies.

Governments have sometimes tended to intervene in the vertical supply chain for television to prevent excessive dominance of the industry. In the US, for example, interventions were made through what were called the Financial Interest and Syndication or 'Finsyn' rules (Owen and Wildman, 1992: 202). These are restrictions which, from 1970 until 1995, limited the extent of vertical integration between what were then the three major television broadcast networks (ABC, CBS and NBC) and content-makers mostly based in Hollywood (Litman, 1998: 142). The Finsyn rules limited the extent to which the networks were allowed to share in any profits from secondary sales of the programmes they aired, thus effectively preventing these three large corporations from getting involved in the television production business.

A similar kind of regulatory intervention was introduced more recently in the UK. As discussed in Chapter 6, the main television broadcasters in the UK have been required, since 1990, to purchase around a quarter of their programming output from television production companies that are 'independent' – i.e. not owned by themselves or any other broadcaster.

Interventions of this sort are intended to prevent powerful vertically integrated broadcasting entities from monopolizing the entire supply chain for television. Policy-makers have sought to increase competition within programme-making and to provide opportunities for the content production sector to develop separately from the broadcasting sector. Even so, the high level of vertical cross-ownership of UK television broadcasting and programme production within the sample group seems indicative of the (at least, perceived) benefits of being involved in both creating and distributing television content.

When the performance of the six programme-makers in the UK sample is ranked according to profitability, a contradictory picture begins to emerge as to whether 'independent' producers fare better or worse than their vertically integrated rivals: see Figure 5.2. Both the highest (Pearson)

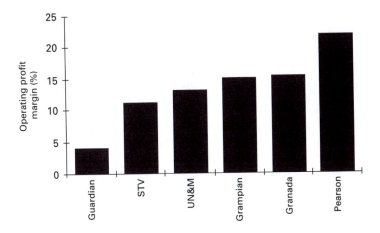

FIGURE 5.2  Operating profit margins for UK television production sample in 1996

and the lowest (Guardian Media Group) operating margins in this sample group are achieved, respectively, by the two independent production companies. So, at first glance, it would appear that the correlation between size and performance discussed in the previous chapter is stronger than any association between vertical structure and performance.

This limited quantitative evidence suggests that UK television production companies who are vertically integrated into broadcasting may achieve a steadier, although not necessarily better, economic performance than those who are 'independent'. A number of theoretical explanations would account for this trend, including the notion first advanced by Coase (1937) and later developed by Williamson (1975; Williamson and Winter, 1993) that where inter-firm transactions in the marketplace are characterized by uncertainty, an incentive for vertical integration will be the opportunity to reduce risk – a 'transaction cost'.

Qualitative research based on this sample of UK television production companies has allowed the implications of vertical expansion to be scrutinized more closely. Technological interdependence between production and distribution is evidently not a special feature of the television industry. On the other hand, a certain level of in-house programme production activity is understood by some UK television companies to be essential to the fulfilment of the terms of their broadcasting licences. This is true only to the extent that a broadcaster's requirements cannot be supplied by the external market – if, for instance, there were not enough 'independent' programme-makers available in the broadcaster's region to supply it, at an appropriate cost, with the programmes needed under the terms of its broadcasting licence. Whether, on the whole, the degree of vertical integration exhibited by UK broadcasters reflects (or is justified by) a shortage of competing programme suppliers seems questionable. Even so, the notion that vertical integration is a *de facto* licence requirement is still widely propagated by some UK terrestrial broadcasters. Thus, according to one Chief Executive of a regional ITV company:

> Overhead recovery is the big advantage [of vertical integration]. You can't have half a camera or half a studio. If you're going to have a studio – and you've *got* to have a studio – then let's fill that studio as many days of the week and as many hours of the day as you can.

Efficiency gains are sometimes not easily disentangled from the market power advantages of vertical expansion. The increased control over the market enjoyed by vertically integrated television companies may be precisely what gives rise to some efficiency gains. For example, the vertically integrated production firm has a very significant advantage over the 'independent' producer in terms of managing capacity efficiently. Vertical integration ensures a given level of demand from the related broadcasting operation whereas 'independent suppliers [must] bear the brunt of demand fluctuations' (George et al., 1992: 74).

The managers of both independent and vertically integrated UK television production companies acknowledge that a steady or predictable flow of output is important in terms of optimizing the use of fixed overheads. Thus, a stark contrast between the operating profit margins achieved by an 'independent' production company (e.g. Guardian Media Group's subsidiary) and a vertically integrated production company (e.g. Grampian Television) at, broadly, the same level of market share may be accounted for by efficiencies in capacity management on the part of the latter.

Production efficiencies can be gained by vertically integrated production companies through overlapping use of resources for 'in-house' as well as externally commissioned work, and through a higher level of knowledge concerning their own rate of output. In theory, 'independent' producers could benefit equally from production efficiencies if they also enjoyed an assured level of demand for their output. In practice, some independent producers who have become established as 'important suppliers' (e.g. Pearson) are able to sustain a steady production slate, but most are faced with highly unpredictable demand. Qualitative findings suggest that the crucial advantage of shared ownership over both these stages is that resources which are indivisible (and, typically, seen as partly integral to the broadcasting function) will be exploited more consistently and at more cost-efficient levels.

While efficiency gains are undeniably an advantage of vertical integration, the pursuit of market power represents another highly evident motive for production companies and television broadcasters to join forces. Integrated firms can, to some extent, avoid the market power of dominant buyers. In addition, producer-broadcasters have an informational advantage over their 'independent' rivals which can help them to get positioned to secure new orders for programmes. As one vertically integrated producer-broadcaster explains: 'There is absolutely no doubt that being part of ITV [broadcasting] gets the intelligence to you faster. It would be daft to pretend otherwise.'

Market power is a crucial factor in the economics of programme supply. As discussed in the previous chapter, an 'important' supplier secures bargaining power which can be used to gain additional programme commissions and better terms of trade. Thus, from a broadcaster's point of view, excessive reliance on a small number of important suppliers may create the possibility of post-contractual opportunistic behaviour on the part of these suppliers. If the supplier of a key programme in a broadcaster's schedule threatens to withdraw that programme or to sell it at a higher price to a rival broadcaster, then high costs may have to be incurred to retain that particular programme. Vertical integration provides a way of avoiding the higher costs associated with such behaviour.

In summary, the experiences of this sample of UK television production companies suggests that while vertical expansion from programme production to broadcasting or vice versa will create some significant efficiencies and benefits, it is not absolutely essential for the success of a programme production company. Several 'independent' production firms have managed to prove their ability to conceive and supply 'hit' programmes and consequently have become key players in the UK television industry. But, because levels of demand for new programmes tend to be uncertain and because of the complexities or attendant transaction costs associated with leasing out any spare capacity, the additional security that vertically integrated firms gain – the knowledge that access to distribution is assured for a certain quantity of output – is generally a big advantage and allows them the opportunity to operate more cost-efficiently.

## Convergence, cross-media expansion and economic performance

The experiences and managerial perspectives offered by this sample of leading UK media firms confirm that *some* and, indeed, very many combinations of cross-media ownership unambiguously provide synergies and cost-efficiencies. Different combinations of diagonal cross-ownership yield different sorts of efficiency gains. For example, expansion from print to electronic publishing offers plentiful opportunity to share or 'repurpose' specialist content between these two different text-based activities. Likewise, diagonal mergers of magazine and newspaper publishers can offer operational synergies. Efficiency gains are also possible, to some extent, through sharing of production and transmission resources between radio and television (as exemplified by the 'bi-media' approach introduced at the BBC in the 1990s).

However, as far as economic efficiency is concerned, there is relatively little to recommend combined ownership of television broadcasting plus newspaper publishing activities. This finding is crucial since it flatly contradicts the main argument in favour of liberalizing cross-media ownership restrictions. The general thrust of arguments favouring deregulation of UK cross-ownership rules has been that technological developments ('convergence') have created new operational synergies between the newspaper and television industries. This argument is incorporated within the UK Government's proposals, of May 1995, for relaxing cross-media restrictions:

> Technological change and convergence provide the opportunity for newspapers, broadcasters and production companies to apply their traditional expertise in new and complementary areas . . .
> Alliances between television and newspaper companies are a logical and natural product of the economic and technological dynamics of the industry and will allow a healthy interchange of skills and creativity for the benefit of the consumer . . . The similarity of functions which newspapers and broadcasters undertake in terms of collecting, editing and disseminating information, news and entertainment, means that there are obvious and natural synergies between companies within each sector, and that it is in the interests of both the industry and the consumer to allow larger media companies to develop. (DNH, 1995a: 19–20)

The claim that common ownership of television and newspapers creates specific cost-efficiencies or other tangible economic benefits is comprehensively challenged by the findings of empirical research. Several firms in the UK sample group are involved in both newspaper publishing and television and none have seen evidence of the 'logical and natural' synergies alluded to above. The best economic case in favour of cross-ownership would appear to be the potential for as yet undeveloped markets for 'multi'-media products to emerge – a much more tentative proposition.

Despite the spread of digital technologies, the skills, techniques and equipment involved in newspaper production and distribution are, in fact, generally still quite *different* from those required in the television industry, and vice versa. So, combining these activities under common ownership will not necessarily create any special efficiency gains or opportunities to rationalize resources. Unless there is a strong shared focus between services, then there is little economic incentive for seeking to combine these activities. Consequently, diversified media conglomerates such as News Corporation often allow broadcasting and newspaper subsidiaries to operate in almost complete isolation from each other.

One special feature of cross-owning television and newspapers is, however, the opportunity it creates to cross-promote the firm's products. Whether this feature is economically beneficial or damaging depends on how it is used. When cross-promotion is used to facilitate *de novo* expansion (i.e. the introduction of new products which increase choice) then welfare and competition should be enhanced (Moschandreas, 1994: 349). For example, if a media conglomerate uses the pages of its newspapers to attract attention to and promote the launch of a new television service that adds to competition and viewer choice then, arguably, cross-promotion is economically beneficial. On the other hand, if the conglomerate uses cross-promotion to build cross-sectoral dominance for its existing media products then this will have a negative impact on competition and on pluralism.

Risk-reduction is another potential benefit associated with diagonal expansion. The UK national newspaper industry provides a clear example of a sector which is in slow decline while, at the same time, subscription television and electronic media are perceived as growth areas. Another possible motivation underlying strategies of cross-media expansion is the desire to exploit anticipated synergies. For example, the expectation that growth in electronic communications will stimulate demand for new products based on both audiovisual images and text has been cited as a factor encouraging diagonal mergers between UK television broadcasters and newspaper publishing companies. And of course motives other than profit maximization – i.e. managerial motives – may also play a role in cross-media mergers.

In analysing the economic gains that arise from any strategy of diagonal expansion, it is important to distinguish between different sorts of advantages – efficiency gains versus risk-spreading, etc. – and between different potential beneficiaries – the firm's shareholders, or its managers or society at large. The achievement of efficiency gains (e.g. economies or scale and scope) will not only serve the interests of the firm but should also contribute to the wider good of the economy by engendering an improved use of resources. Strategies of cross-media expansion that yield no efficiency gains and are predicated solely on the strategic interests of the firm's shareholders or managers will not give rise to any general economic gains.

On the contrary, the accumulation of greater size, more market power and dominant market positions can lead to behaviour and practices which run contrary to the public interest (Moschandreas, 1994: 483–4). Once a firm achieves a dominant position, the removal of competitive pressures may give rise to various inefficiencies, including excessive expenditure of resources aimed simply at maintaining dominance. Hence, as discussed in Chapter 3, public policy interventions are required to promote sufficient competition to induce firms to operate efficiently.

As far as vertical expansion is concerned, it is easy to see the strategic attractions for a media firm of a corporate structure that gives it control over both content production and distribution. As a distributor, vertical expansion 'upstream' into production means that you have an assured supply of appropriate content to disseminate through your distribution infrastructure. As a content producer, vertical integration with a distributor means assured access to audiences. The wider the distribution of media content, the lower its (per-consumer) production costs will be. In television, per-viewer production costs can be reduced by 'selling' the same output to as many different audiences or segments of the audience as possible.

Vertical integration is a common strategy amongst the sample of UK television companies. A desire for more security or more control over the marketplace is a central underlying motive. But another advantage evident from the experience of the UK sample group is that vertical expansion can reduce 'transaction costs'. For example, broadcasters who internalize the programme production process rather than purchasing programme rights in the open market may face fewer complications, delays, etc. in securing exactly the sort of content they require.

So, as with other forms of corporate expansion, the two main incentives associated with vertical growth are improved efficiency and the accumulation of market power. In any example of vertical expansion, both motives may be present and, indeed, 'the two are not unrelated' (George et al., 1992: 65). Vertical integration may be motivated by the desire to minimize costs or by the wish for greater security (e.g. access to essential raw materials such as, for a broadcaster, attractive television programming) but then the latter – the desire to gain some control over the market environment – may itself result in market dominance.

The potential for cost reductions within a vertically integrated firm may stem from improved information – for example, about price or product specifications or, more generally, about the market. In the television industry, the costs (created by uncertainty, weaker informational flows, etc.) involved in inter-firm trade between programme producers and broadcasters may well be higher than when both activities are carried out in-house. It may save time and hassle to be able to source the pro-grammes that are needed directly from an in-house production division rather than having to shop around, negotiate and make deals with external programme-makers.

But, for media firms, strategic factors often play a more important role in encouraging expansion across different phases in the supply chain: a broadcaster that has to rely on external producers to supply all the 'hit' programmes in its schedule will find itself vulnerable to the market power of producers. If monopoly power is present in the programme production stage (say, because a supplier has control over a specific programme for which no perceived substitutes are available) then, even without vertical integration, the firm with upstream monopoly power may be able to appropriate some of any monopoly profits available at the broadcast-ing stage (Moschandreas, 1994: 417). It is rarely the situation that no substitutes are available for a particular product but, with television programming, specificity of inputs (particular actors, sportsmen, writers or presenters) is a factor in their popularity and success. So, to avoid being held to ransom by important suppliers, broadcasters and other media distributors may choose to expand vertically into production.

From a content-producer's point of view, vertical integration also offers numerous strategic attractions. Ownership of, say, a broadcaster or a video distributor ensures that the firm's output will find its way to audiences. Vertical integration may lead to a more predictable and reliable stream of orders. A steady production slate is a major advantage. It allows the vertically integrated production firm to plan more effectively and to use its production resources – equipment, technicians, personnel, etc. – more efficiently. Assured distribution also helps the vertically integrated producer to build up a reputation or a strong brand name as a supplier of programmes.

An example of another sort of vertical merger in the media industry was provided recently by Time Warner and America Online (AOL). Time Warner is a major producer of news and entertainment and owns a huge library of media content, and it also runs the second largest US cable network. America Online is the largest Internet service provider (ISP) in the US with some 26 million subscribers. The potential gains for Time Warner/AOL from bringing together strengths both in content creation and in online distribution are very promising. On the other hand, the dangers posed to rivals by allowing such a powerful vertically integrated entity to take shape were summed up in a *Financial Times* editorial as follows: 'The combined group could harm other content providers by restricting access to AOL subscribers and damage other ISPs by denying them access to Time Warner content' (2001: 22).

So, as with other forms of corporate expansion, the two main incentives associated with vertical growth are improved efficiency and the accumulation of market power. In any example of vertical expansion, both motives may be present and, indeed, 'the two are not unrelated' (George et al., 1992: 65). It is sometimes very difficult to disentangle the pursuit of greater efficiency and greater security from the pursuit of monopoly power. Vertical integration may appear to be motivated by the desire to minimize costs or by the wish for greater security (e.g. access to essential raw materials such as, for a broadcaster, attractive television programming) but then the latter – the desire to gain some control over the market environment – may itself result in a position of dominance.

On the basis of the findings considered here, it seems that the desire for greater control over the market environment is uppermost in decisions to expand vertically. However, the more control that any media firm acquires across additional stages in the vertical supply chain, the more danger there is that it will start to dominate the market, with detrimental consequences for rivals and consumers. Vertical integration can sometimes protect the market power of incumbent firms by raising barriers to entry. So, although most media firms might want freedom to expand across all stages in the vertical supply chain, there is also a powerful public interest case in favour of restraining (or at least monitoring) vertical expansion so as to sustain market access and promote fair and effective competition.

As regards diagonal cross-ownership, on the basis of the findings considered here there is little evidence that cross-ownership of broadcasting plus newspaper publishing is likely to yield significant efficiency gains or that it would contribute positively to economic welfare. Many combinations of cross-ownership should provide valuable synergies and cost-efficiencies but, according to the experiences of leading UK media firms, this is not necessarily true of broadcasting plus newspaper ownership. So, even though such cross-ownership might suit the private or strategic interests of individual media firms, there is no compelling public interest case in favour of encouraging such corporate configurations. On the contrary, conglomerate expansion or empire-building in the media, as in any other sector of industry, will tend to trigger economic policy concerns related to the need to preserve competition and prevent abuses of market power.

# Media Ownership Policy
# – The UK Case

# 6

# The Development of Regulation and Policy

## Evolution of UK media ownership policy

> Undue concentration or abuses of market power are normally addressed under competition legislation . . . However, wider objectives are important as far as the media are concerned. A free and diverse media are an indispensable part of the democratic process [sic]. They provide the multiplicity of voices and opinions that informs the public, influences opinion, and engenders political debate. They promote the culture of dissent which any healthy democracy must have. In so doing, they contribute to the cultural fabric of the nation and help define our sense of identity and purpose. If one voice becomes too powerful, this process is placed in jeopardy and democracy is damaged. Special media ownership rules, which exist in all major media markets, are needed therefore to provide the safeguards necessary to maintain diversity and plurality. (DNH, 1995a: 3)

The above extract from the 1995 Green Paper on media ownership explains the need, as perceived by the UK Government, for special rules aimed specifically at restricting levels of media and cross-media ownership. This need has been recognized in UK law for some time and public concerns about the adverse effects of excessive concentrations of media ownership can be traced back to the first Royal Commission on the Press of 1949. That first Royal Commission (a public inquiry) into the conduct of the press concluded that levels of media concentration, although high at the time, were not a threat to the public interest. Its findings, according to Ralph Negrine, 'have been heavily criticised ever since' (1994: 62). Nonetheless, specific legislation aimed at curbing the development of media empires was soon to follow.

A series of additional public inquiries into the behaviour and structure of the UK newspaper industry gave ongoing prominence to, amongst other issues, the problem of excessive concentrations of newspaper ownership

(Seymour-Ure, 1991). As a consequence of concerns about monopolisation of the press, the 1973 Fair Trading Act introduced a special procedure whereby transfers of ownership of newspapers would require the prior consent of the Secretary of State for Trade and Industry. Under certain circumstances, such transfers must be referred to the competition authorities – the Competition Commission (CC) – so that all relevant public interest implications can be examined.

The 1973 Fair Trading Act contains two sets of merger rules: one applying to newspaper mergers and the other applying to all other types of merger. Broadly, the latter serves to limit mergers which have anti-competitive effects that are contrary to the public interest. This test also applies to newspaper mergers but, in relation to newspapers, specific account is taken of 'all matters which appear in the circumstances to be relevant and, in particular, the need for accurate presentation of news and free expression of opinion'.[1]

The 1973 Act sets out a procedure whereby, in any instance of merger or sale of a newspaper where the transfer would result in a single proprietor having combined control over daily circulations in excess of a given threshold, the prior consent of the Secretary of State for Trade is required. Before giving consent, the Secretary of State for Trade is obliged to refer such a transfer to the Monopolies and Mergers Commission (MMC) in order for a test of the public interest implications to be carried out. As indicated above, the wording of the Act is somewhat vague with regard to the criteria for the public interest test and whether, say, the impact on diversity of editorial viewpoints would form a legitimate concern is not clear (Robertson and Nicol, 1992: 506).

An important feature of the Act is that, if the Secretary of State for Trade is satisfied that the newspaper being acquired is 'not economic as a going concern', he or she may give consent for the transfer of ownership to go ahead *without* any referral to the MMC or any independent assessment. In the interests of sustaining the existence of titles which are or appear to be in financial difficulty, the Secretary of State may give unconditional consent for a proprietor to accumulate high levels of newspaper ownership. This apparent loophole is frequently held to blame for 'concentrating a large amount of national newspaper power [in the UK] in one controversial pair of hands' (ibid.: 503) – namely, those of Rupert Murdoch.[2]

In addition to these rules concerning newspaper mergers in the Fair Trading Act, special provisions on ownership of commercial (television and radio) broadcasting licences and on cross-ownership between broadcasting and the newspaper sector have been set out in successive pieces of UK broadcasting legislation. For the most part, ownership rules in broadcasting legislation are designed to place an upper limit on the amount of radio or television broadcasting licences or the level of cross-media ownership anybody may have. The main provisions which existed prior to a major review of UK media ownership policy in 1994–95 were contained in the 1990 Broadcasting Act. This Act stipulated that, in general, individuals and companies from any European Union member state are subject to exactly the same ownership restrictions as UK operators, and these can be summarized briefly as follows. Those deemed eligible for terrestrial television broadcasting licence ownership were permitted to own either (a) two regional ITV (also called C3) licences (but not both of the London licences), or (b) a national ITV licence, or (c) a C5 licence.[3] Ownership of a licence in one category would restrict ownership to a 20 per cent investment in either of the other categories.

The Act set out various restrictions on those who were disqualified from owning either an ITV or C5 licence. Beyond those who are not 'fit and proper', these were non-EU nationals or companies, advertising agencies and religious, political or charitable organizations. Those categorized as unsuitable for ownership of broadcasting licences were restricted under the 1990 Act to holdings of no more than 5 per cent in any UK terrestrial television broadcasting licence.

As regards cross-media ownership, the 1990 Act contained strict rules that prevented national newspaper proprietors from also owning either an ITV or C5 licence. Cross-ownership between newspapers and cable or non-domestic satellite broadcasting was not restricted. But national newspaper proprietors who wanted to diversify into terrestrial broadcasting were restricted to a 20 per cent initial holding and 5 per cent maximum stake in any subsequent investment in a television or national radio licence. Local newspaper proprietors and radio operators were also restricted from cross-ownership of regional television broadcasting in overlapping areas, and vice versa. The 1990 Act provided for a moratorium on takeovers of ITV companies for the first year of operation of the new set of licences commencing in January 1993. This was intended to enable ITV companies to focus solely on their service obligations during the initial phase of their new licences.

The 1990 Act (and secondary legislation) also included a framework for restricting ownership within the commercial radio sector. These rules are based on a market share approach whereby, in general, no single operator is allowed to have more than 15 per cent of the total 'points' allocated to the commercial radio system as a whole. As with restrictions on television licence ownership, the underlying aim of curtailing radio ownership is to promote pluralism and prevent excessive accumulations of power over broadcast media that might pose a threat to the public interest.

In addition, the 1990 Broadcasting Act encouraged some vertical disaggregation of ownership between television broadcasting and television programme production. This was achieved, following an earlier recommendation in the Peacock Report (1986), by imposing on dominant terrestrial broadcasters a compulsory 'independent' access quota – i.e. the obligation to source at least 25 per cent of transmitted output from programme-makers who are independent (not owned by broadcasters). Under secondary legislation – the Broadcasting (Independent Productions) Order 1991 – the permitted holding of a television broadcaster in an 'independent' production company, and vice versa, was set at 15 per cent.

### The cross-media ownership review, 1994–95

One of the outstanding features of UK policy has been its lack of effectiveness in preventing excessive concentrations of, especially, newspaper ownership. This was one of several factors which contributed to the need for a major review of media ownership policy in 1994–95. Table 6.1 provides an indication of the exceptionally high levels of concentrated ownership in the UK national newspaper sector at the time the review was announced.

TABLE 6.1   Share of total UK national newspaper circulations in 1994

| Newspaper group | Share (%) |
| --- | --- |
| News Corporation<br>*The Sun, Today, The Times, News of the World, The Sunday Times* | 37 |
| Mirror Group<br>*Daily Mirror, Daily Record, Sunday Mirror, Sunday Record, The People,*<br>*The Independent, The Independent on Sunday* | 26 |
| United Newspapers<br>*Daily Express, Daily Star, Sunday Express* | 13 |
| Daily Mail and General Trust<br>*Daily Mail, The Mail on Sunday* | 12 |
| The Telegraph plc<br>*Daily Telegraph, Sunday Telegraph* | 7 |
| Guardian Media Group plc<br>*The Guardian, The Observer* | 3 |
| Pearson plc<br>*Financial Times* | 1 |

*Source:* ABC, reproduced in Green Paper on media ownership (DNH, 1995a: 33)

The first suggestion that a review of cross-ownership policy should be carried out came in October 1993 from the Independent Television Commission, the body responsible for regulating UK commercial broadcasters. The review was suggested in the context of a proposal from the ITC to extend the temporary moratorium on ITV takeovers. The Government rejected the notion of extending ITV's protection from takeovers but agreed to a review and also decided to do away with the 'penny farthing' principle which had previously prevented anyone from owning two 'large' regional ITV licences.[4]

This decision paved the way for a virtually instant transformation in ITV ownership configurations. Immediately following the Government's announcement, Central ITV (ITV licence holder for the Midlands) was acquired by Carlton Television (holder of the London weekday licence), LWT (holder of the London weekend ITV licence) was subject to a hostile takeover by Granada Group (holder of the North-West licence) and Anglia (holder of the East of England licence) was acquired by MAI (holder of the South-East of England ITV licence). As ITV began to consolidate, the question of appropriate structures for the control of media ownership in the UK came to the forefront.

The debate surrounding the announcement that UK media ownership rules would be subject to a major review instantly gave voice to industrial concerns, particularly from the newspaper sector, about the strategic position of the UK's existing organizations in a more competitive and international media marketplace. In line with the message being sent from industry to Government in many other countries, UK policy-makers were assailed by arguments that existing restrictions on media ownership had been overtaken by events in the media world of the 1990s (DNH, 1995a: 11).

A clear international tendency towards increased vertical expansion and concentration of media ownership around this time had also triggered the same policy question in other European countries such as France and Germany, as well as at the collective EU level and in the United States (MacLeod, 1996). Uncertainty prevailed as to whether national and international regulators would see fit to encourage or prevent their own indigenous media organizations from joining this trend. At every level, including that of the European Union (CEC, 1994), debate was being driven by industrial calls for deregulation which were at odds with traditional socio-political and cultural concerns about preserving pluralism.

The UK Cross-Media Ownership Review Committee was led by the Department of National Heritage (DNH) – since re-named the Department of Culture, Media and Sport (DCMS) – and it commenced work in January

1994. It took as its starting point the policy approach favoured by the then Minister for National Heritage, Peter Brook. Mr Brook was in favour of maintaining restraints to curb excessive concentrations of media ownership – an objective which had not been achieved entirely satisfactorily under existing legislation. However, Mr Brook was succeeded in the role of Secretary of State for National Heritage at a relatively early stage during the Cross-Media Ownership Review by Stephen Dorrell, who introduced a significantly different approach. Contrary to his predecessor, Dorrell's 'free market' approach tended to be in strong sympathy with the arguments and aspirations of large industrial players for a comprehensive liberalization of existing media ownership rules.

Even so, deregulatory impulses could not easily be squared with the objective of preserving pluralism and, for some people, preserving diversity in the media was as important an objective for public policy as it had ever been. In fact, the failure of existing legislation to prevent excessive concentrations of ownership was a recurrent theme in the public debate about media ownership policy. The accumulation of a very significant share of the UK media by one particular player – News International – was seen by some as, in itself, a prime justification for reviewing existing ownership rules and, indeed, as an argument for strengthening their effectiveness.

Another concern – supported more widely and by a much more politically influential constituency – was that existing rules posed a threat to the survival and development of commercially successful indigenous media firms. Ownership restrictions which are designed to promote domestic plurality also, it was argued, tend to militate against the maximization of economies of scale and scope. Non-domestic organizations that *can* achieve such economies are better placed to expand into new markets and compete cost-effectively. So, according to several media organizations, in an expanded and internationalized economy, existing constraints on the size of UK industry participants represented a handicap which was undermining their competitive position.

Even so, liberalizing impulses were also accompanied by risk. Any relaxation in UK cross-ownership restrictions which allowed the consolidation and rationalization of domestic media interests (and applied non-discriminatorily to EU organizations) would also bolster the prospective returns from UK market participation for non-domestic rivals. At a time when overseas expansion for UK media firms was bedevilled by wide disparities in media ownership restrictions across other EU member states, any policy change which would provide non-reciprocal access to *increased* UK media ownership might appear ill-judged.

The Cross-Media Ownership Review Committee took a lengthy period – some 18 months – before arriving at any policy proposals. With much pressure for a UK policy change to allow enlarged media cross-holdings, and in the face of a growing number of mergers and strategic alliances at home and abroad, there was little will, in some political quarters, to take account of pluralism or diversity of media ownership as objectives. In fact, keeping pluralism on the policy agenda at all posed considerable challenges for the Review Committee. However, 'economic' arguments in favour of liberalization proved difficult to resist, not least because of the political strength of the voices which were supporting this case.

The submissions received by the DNH in spring 1994 – prominent amongst which were the views of large media companies – provide a useful insight to the various conflicting objectives that the Review Committee was somehow supposed to reconcile. The parties most clearly interested in the outcome of the review were UK media industry participants, especially large newspaper proprietors lobbying for greater flexibility, and their views were widely represented in evidence to the Committee. The public interest case for maintaining existing ownership restrictions to protect pluralism was generally put forward by smaller regional media operators, lobby groups and trade unions. Advertisers also supported diverse media ownership on an agenda of commercial self-interest.

In favour of liberalization, Pearson plc, for example, argued that existing cross-ownership restrictions were out of step with the current media environment; they were forcing investors to choose between delivery and production and preventing 'natural' commercial alliances developing. The UK newspaper market is declining and, with new more profitable media segments developing, Pearson and others wanted the flexibility to 'grow and expand globally from a sound domestic base' (Pearson, 1994). The key to the future, it was argued, is the interrelationship of media, electronics, computers and telecoms. The race to globalised integrated media companies was on and, if a UK firm was to be among the top six or seven global companies expected to dominate the industry as a result of continued consolidation over coming years, the UK Government must relax ownership rules.

Pearson's views were echoed in evidence from the highly influential British Media Industry Group (BMIG) which comprised Associated Newspapers, the Guardian Media Group and the Telegraph plc, as well as Pearson again. The BMIG suggested that UK cross-ownership restrictions needed to be abolished to give publishers the right to diversify 'into the new multinational and multimedia market' (BMIG, 1994). It acknowledged that newspapers are in long-term decline compared with the rest of the media and suggested that deregulation of cross-media ownership rules was essential if Britain was to take advantage of the multimedia revolution.

The theme of adopting a 'market share' approach to the measurement of media ownership was taken up in the Independent Television Commission's evidence to the Committee. According to the ITC, 'basing ownership restrictions on the holding of a particular number of licences without regard to their economic significance is no longer consistent with developments in commercial television' (ITC, 1994). A market share approach might create problems in defining percentage shareholdings in a transparent way, but it would be better suited to the new multichannel environment. The ITC acknowledged the continuing need for cross-ownership restrictions to maintain editorial diversity, but was broadly in favour of some relaxation and correction of current rules.

On the issue of pluralism, the ITC suggested that 'the more obvious dangers in cross holding can be avoided' provided that the public interest requirements of accuracy and due impartiality and the prevention of editorializing by licensed broadcasters continued to apply. On the other hand, it went on to say that 'the possibility of undesirable dominance through agenda setting, as distinct from matters of accuracy and due impartiality, remains an issue which should continue to be addressed by retaining specific limitations on ownership'.

In contrast with lines of economic argument submitted by industry participants, evidence from the Centre for Communication and Information Studies (CCIS) at the University of Westminster opened by making the point that 'existing cross-media ownership restrictions in the UK are primarily political rather than economic in aim'. These restrictions are concerned with ensuring pluralism and, for such plurality to exist, media players must be economically viable. However, the public interest case for current restrictions should not be abandoned unless there is strong evidence that current ownership structures are economically unsustainable.

Such evidence, according to the CCIS, was not to be found. The impact of globalization and convergence had been greatly exaggerated – many media products were still largely confined to their own national or regional markets and cross-media synergy was 'largely a myth', so it was not clear that the multimedia conglomerate is the optimum model (Garnham and Porter, 1994). The arrival of broadband digital networks delivering a range of multimedia services, which would require quite different regulatory structures, was still some 20 years away. Meanwhile, the competitive threat to a fragmented ITV had also been exaggerated. So, according to the CCIS, existing restrictions on cross-media ownership ought to be maintained. Much of the pressure for this review had arisen, in fact, from the anomaly of News International's dominant position in the UK newspaper and satellite television markets. But rather than removing cross-ownership rules to create a level playing field, ownership of satellite broadcasting should be brought within existing restrictions.

The Campaign for Press and Broadcasting Freedom (CPBF – a campaign group for 'a diverse, democratic and accountable media') was also sceptical about the hype surrounding multimedia and convergence and it argued that wider considerations of the role of media in a democratic society should be at the centre of any balanced review of media ownership. The CPBF's submission emphasized the need to protect diversity of opinion and the potentially adverse consequences of allowing inordinate media power to accumulate in the hands of single individuals or organizations. The CPBF suggested that 'market forces will not lead to diversity of opinion and expression; Governments have to ensure a regulatory framework to encourage that' (Williams, 1994). It argued for tighter restrictions on cross-media ownership including the principle of 'one owner, one outlet' to cover national newspapers, national radio stations, satellite television and C3.

The Institute of Practitioners in Advertising (IPA), which represents the major part of the UK advertising agency business, was also in favour of a plurality in media outlets. However, the concern expressed in its evidence was not with ensuring plurality and diversity of information for the public, but with ensuring open competition and freedom of choice for advertisers to place their advertisements cost-effectively in appropriate media.

A number of trade unions submitted evidence to the Committee on Cross-Media Ownership: all of them expressed concern with the need for strict rules to maintain diverse UK media ownership and pluralism. The National Union of Journalists (NUJ) pointed out that pressure for existing restrictions to be lifted had come principally from the self-serving arguments of newspaper groups who wished to move into newer and potentially more profitable electronic media, but 'case studies' of Rupert Murdoch and Silvio Berlusconi demonstrate the dangers of excessive media concentration. The NUJ suggested that 'without national, pan-European and transnational regulation, there is a real danger that tomorrow's information super highway will be hogged by a small bunch of media juggernauts who will bear down on smaller competitors, who challenge their pre-eminent position' (NUJ, 1994). Therefore, existing cross-ownership restrictions should not only be maintained but extended to cable and satellite television.

According to the Broadcasting, Entertainment, Cinematograph and Theatre Union (BECTU), the weakness of some of the arguments for deregulation as the strategy for surviving in 'the multimedia market' was their excessive reliance on commercial rather than broader cultural considerations. Concerns with the need for diversity, representativeness and freedom of expression in the media and for a plurality of views and interests to be expressed should not be ignored. 'An understandable concern to provide and protect UK commercial interests in media hardware and technology need not and should not be a reason for undermining a commitment to pluralism in programming' (BECTU, 1994). BECTU recommended that, in the short term, existing cross-ownership restrictions should be maintained, except for amendments to ensure that News International was made subject to the same regulations as other companies. Until the development of European policy in this area becomes clearer, it would be unwise for the UK to significantly relax ownership restrictions.

Weighing up the key positions that were represented to the DNH during the 1994–95 review process, it is clear that considerable pressure was mounted for amendments which would allow UK media companies to expand their domestic positions as they see fit. Arguments in favour of relaxing existing ownership rules were in keeping with the free market approach favoured by the then Conservative Government and by the Minister for National Heritage. But liberalizing influences had to be measured against sacrificing plurality and diversity in the media. If pluralism meant anything as a social policy objective, it would be difficult to justify doing away with curbs on excessive domestic media concentrations simply in order to generate undesirable concentrations of UK media power at the international level.

Precisely the same dilemma – a conflict between pro-liberalization industrial arguments and concerns to preserve pluralism – has been facing media ownership policy-makers in many other European countries and at the collective level of the European Union. Several consultation exercises carried out by the European Commission, following on from its Green Paper (CEC: 1992) *Pluralism and Media Concentration in the Internal Market*, have revealed almost exactly the same battle lines within the European policy debate on media ownership.

Some of the strongest voices in the European debate have been, as in the UK, those of media organizations who want to be allowed to grow large enough to compete effectively with major integrated rivals from other member states and elsewhere. It is not always clear whether their exhortations are aimed at equalizing restrictions across Europe in the interests of fair and equal competition, or simply at liberalizing their own domestic ownership rules to give indigenous operators some kind of a head start. At the level of each individual state, arguments in favour of a more liberal ownership regime are often expressed in terms of the need to match the competitiveness of European media rivals. Similarly, at the European level, greater flexibility is argued for on the basis that the European audiovisual industry encounters great external competition from the American and Japanese industries.

At every level, there are strong and understandable sensitivities about the need to sustain an economically viable indigenous media industry, and the fear of losing competitiveness to foreign rivals has been deployed extensively and judiciously by companies with an obvious commercial self-interest in expansion.

Like the European Commission, the UK Cross-Media Ownership Review Committee was expected somehow to perform a balancing act between the various interests and policy objectives which would be affected by whatever stance it were to adopt on media ownership. Unlike the Commission, which has yet to find any acceptable resolution of the conflicting aims and arguments, the UK Cross-Media Ownership Review Committee duly delivered its policy proposals in the summer of 1995.

For UK policy-makers, the political influence of certain media owners played a crucial role in determining how the conflict between 'pro' and 'anti' liberalization arguments was resolved. The British Media Industry Group (BMIG) – a lobby organized by most national newspaper publishers, but excluding News International and Mirror Group Newspapers – was particularly influential (Snoddy, 1995a, 1995b). It would seem that, above all else, the Government was keen to secure this group's approval for its policy recommendations. Consequently, the aspirations of this constituency are heavily imprinted on the proposals that were eventually arrived at. A leading member of the Review Committee acknowledged the importance of the BMIG in the following terms:

> I think undoubtedly the campaign that the BMIG waged was extremely persuasive, and it obviously suited Ministers *politically* to be able to accommodate them ... The BMIG was clearly a self-interested case, undoubtedly ... What can I say? These were political decisions at root.

## The 1995 Green Paper on media ownership

The Secretary of State for National Heritage announced the Government's new framework for regulating media ownership in May 1995. These ideas, presented in a Green Paper (DNH, 1995a), were broadly well received, not only by media industry participants and regulators but also by opposition political parties. The Government's suggestions involved two stages. In the long term, it wanted to sweep away the complexities of the existing media ownership regime and replace it with a new approach based on a company's share of what was adjudged to constitute the 'total' UK media market. According to the Government, an approach which recognized and placed a common upper limit on any media operator's collective media power seemed to offer a more coherent basis for ensuring pluralism. Views were invited on how such an approach might be implemented in the longer term. In the meantime, a number of proposals to adjust and loosen up specific aspects of the existing media ownership regime would be enacted either immediately or during the following parliamentary session.

Plans for immediate action were concerned, first, with a relaxation of the rules on ownership of commercial radio licences. Under the new proposals, the points system[5] for radio would remain and (as before) no company would be allowed to control licences covering more than 15 per cent of the commercial market, but the number of local radio licences which one company could own was increased from 20 to 35 and restrictions on some licence categories were to be removed. These relatively modest adjustments were enacted through secondary legislation and brought about a flurry of corporate activity in the radio sector, involving companies such as Metro, Capital and Chrysalis.[6]

Another of the Government's early actions was to raise the permitted upper-level of cross-ownership between 'independent' television programme producers and broadcasters from the existing 15 per cent of equity up to 25 per cent.[7] This signalled an interesting reversal of the position previously adopted by the Government when, following the 1986 Peacock Report, it was considered that vertically integrated broadcasting companies were stifling the growth of a strong independent programme-making industry in the UK. Now, it seemed, higher levels of cross-investment would actually strengthen the independent production sector. Whether those producers who, under the enactment of the new proposals, benefited from more significant cross-ownership with a broadcaster could still be truly regarded as independent is another matter.

The most significant of the Government's short-term proposals involved substantial amendments to the Broadcasting Act 1990 to relax monomedia and cross-media television and newspaper ownership rules. These would be dealt with under a new Broadcasting Act in the 1995–96 parliamentary session. The proposed changes would establish a shared upper limit on ownership for terrestrial, cable and satellite television operators alike at 15 per cent of the total UK television market, as measured by audience share figures which include the BBC. Commercial television operators would be allowed to control up to a 15 per cent share of the total audience, regardless of delivery method/s involved or the number of channels owned, except that the existing stipulation that no company may own more than two ITV licences would remain unchanged. In other words, ITV companies were to be allowed to own cable and satellite operators, and vice versa, for the first time. As a safeguard, ownership of terrestrial television would be restricted for any cable or satellite company which, in turn, is controlled by a major national newspaper proprietor.

More generally, newspaper groups with less than a 20 per cent share of national circulations (in practice, all but News International and Mirror Group Newspapers) were to be allowed to control up to 15 per cent of the total television market and 15 per cent of the commercial radio market. These new rules were reciprocal so, likewise, television and radio operators may control up to a 20 per cent share of national newspaper circulations as well as up to 15 per cent of the total television market and 15 per cent of the commercial radio markets. To protect diversity at a regional level, newspaper operators with more than a 30 per cent share of circulations in any particular area would not be allowed to own regional television or radio licences in that same region.

The Government's new proposals provided quite significant scope for expansion both within and across the various sectors of the media for virtually all UK newspaper, television and radio operators. They promised most newspaper operators freedom to diversify and derive revenues in the lucrative terrestrial television market and they offered ITV companies the opportunity to invest in cable, satellite, newspapers, radio and (to a greater extent) independent producers. The Green Paper was warmly welcomed by television operators such as Carlton, Granada and MAI, and by the large newspaper groups such as Associated Newspapers, Pearson, the Guardian Media Group and the Telegraph who had been the principal activists in lobbying for a relaxation in media ownership rules.

Another apparent victory for the lobbying efforts of those newspaper groups who comprised the British Media Industry Group was the Government's longer-term proposal of switching to a single media market share or, as the BMIG had suggested, a 'share of voice' approach as the basis for setting ownership restrictions in future (BMIG, 1995). Such an approach had also been advocated, in one form or another, by other companies such as LWT (London Weekend Television) and by the ITC.

A market share approach certainly seemed to offer a fairer and more effective means of curbing media ownership than the previous approach based on limiting the number or type of 'products' (i.e. radio or television licences) owned by a single operator. After all, different newspaper titles, television channels and radio stations command very different levels of impact or control over public opinion. To maintain a diversity of media sources and scope for a plurality of viewpoints, all manifestations of media control must be properly measured and taken account of. In practice, however, the task of weighing up the relative impact of different sorts of media and of devising an acceptable 'exchange rate' to reflect differentials between the influence wielded by different media proved to be highly contentious matters.

At the same time as giving ground to most media players' requests for flexibility, the Government did not submit to suggestions that media ownership be deregulated and governed by competition legislation alone. Notwithstanding new technological and market developments, the need for diversified domestic ownership to be preserved through special media ownership rules was restated and underlined (DNH, 1995a: 3). But the new proposals included no suggestion for action in respect of voices which had already become extremely powerful: no proposals were put forward to set an upper limit on monomedia ownership in the newspaper sector.

The Government's stated aims – to protect pluralism while also setting a framework which allows commercial media operators to take advantage of market opportunities – were set out again in a further Green Paper entitled *Digital Terrestrial Broadcasting* published in August (DNH, 1995b). Under new proposals, six blocks of frequencies or 'multiplexes', each capable of transmitting at least three high-quality terrestrial digital television channels reaching 60–90 per cent of the UK population, would be awarded by the ITC in an open competition in a couple of years' time. In keeping with the proposed new regulatory arrangements for television ownership prescribed in the earlier Green Paper on media ownership, digital broadcasters would be allowed to own any number of digital channels (although not accounting for more than 25 per cent of digital terrestrial frequencies) subject to a ceiling on total television market share of 15 per cent. Multiplex ownership would be restricted to two per company.

Growing concerns in the UK, and also at the European Commission, about the issue of how gatekeepers – primarily, owners of encryption technology for pay-TV and, also, multiplex operators for digital TV – were to be regulated were reflected in both of these Green Papers. *Media Ownership* indicated that those controlling access to encryption technologies and to satellites would be closely monitored by the UK and European competition authorities to ensure that arrangements to supply access to rivals were not anti-competitive. *Digital Terrestrial Broadcasting* went on to propose that providers of encryption or subscription management systems for these new digital services would have to be licensed by the telecommunications regulator (OFTEL) and overseen by the ITC.

Through the Green Paper on media ownership, the Government had invited a further round of public consultation on the means by which media concentration might be measured under its new 'longer-term' market share approach. It also asked for views on who the regulator should be to govern media ownership – whether the ITC, the OFT or some other, perhaps new, agency – and what role that body should play. The Green Paper envisaged that the regulator would be responsible for implementing a public interest test on acquisitions which exceed the common thresholds on media ownership. For the moment, the Government suggested that these thresholds might be fixed at 10 per cent of the total UK media market for any single operator, or 20 per cent of the media market in Scotland, Wales, Northern Ireland and the English regions, or 20 per cent of any one media sector (DNH, 1995a: 24).

Staking a claim to expand its role as the ownership regulator for commercial broadcasting the ITC, in its response, urged the Government to reconsider the proposal put forward in the Green Paper, *Digital Terrestrial Broadcasting* and to award full responsibility for regulating conditional access and subscriber management arrangements to the ITC (ITC, 1995). The Commission maintained that such regulation relates primarily to broadcasting, and so it should be handled by the ITC rather than OFTEL. However, public response to this issue was divided and the Government opted instead to give responsibility for supervision of conditional access providers to the authorities with more experience of competition issues surrounding communications infrastructures: the OFT and, latterly, OFTEL. Nonetheless, the ITC and the Radio Authority were to continue playing a central role in the implementation of media ownership policy. The 1995 Broadcasting Bill gave these bodies responsibility for applying a new public interest test designed to give some special consideration to the general impact – including on pluralism – of mergers between broadcasters and newspapers.

The consultation following the media ownership Green Paper attracted some 70 responses, most of which came from media industry participants who were broadly in support of the liberalizing measures it proposed. However, the main issue raised for consultation was not the key short-term proposal to deregulate television ownership and the cross-ownership of terrestrial television and newspapers but the longer-term proposal to switch to a single media market approach. So the most important revelation from the consultation exercise was that, for most people, a longer-term transfer to a single media market approach, complete with 'exchange rates', seemed unworkable. Consequently, the DNH had little choice other than to abandon these longer-term proposals.

In a way, dropping the proposals for a switch to a share of the 'total' market approach amounted to quite a significant concession. The 1995 Green Paper had envisaged an overall upper limit on ownership of 10 per cent of the total media market for any single supplier. Since, in the short term, monomedia restrictions for radio and television were to be set at some 15 per cent each and there was no proposal to introduce any upper monomedia limits on newspaper ownership, the omission of this overall limit of 10 per cent from the 1995 Broadcasting Bill and from the subsequent 1996 Act meant that any single supplier could now, through cross-sectoral holdings, own well in excess of 10 per cent of the total media market.

A second key policy change conceded between the Green Paper proposals of May 1995 and the publication of the Broadcasting Bill in December 1995 was also deregulatory in its effect. In response to arguments from the major ITV companies that a further round of consolidation of ownership would help them to hold their own in the domestic and international marketplace, the Government decided to abolish the remaining two-licence limit on ITV ownership (with the proviso that the two London licences could not be held in common ownership). Thus, ITV licence holders would be subject to exactly the same upper constraint on ownership as, say, a cable or satellite television provider – i.e. 15 per cent of total television audiences, including the BBC.

Many ITV shareholders benefited from the announcement of this change. Several ITV companies enjoyed 'sharp rises' in share prices on the expectation 'that it would unleash a bidding war for ITV companies' (Financial Times, 1995a: 18; Snoddy, 1995c: 18). The share price of newspaper group United News & Media rose sharply in December 1995 with the publication of the Broadcasting Bill on hopes, which have subsequently proved to be correct, that deregulation of cross-ownership of television and newspapers would help 'find a buyer for the newspaper' (Financial Times, 1995b: 13).

## The 1996 Broadcasting Act: the main provisions

The key proposals which were carried through unscathed from the 1995 Green Paper to the ensuing legislation were those relating to the short term *only*; principally, the deregulation of television ownership and the deregulation of cross-ownership between broadcast and newspaper operators.

The 1996 Act introduced an overall ceiling on monomedia ownership for all television broadcasters, regardless of delivery method or number of licences held. The new common upper ceiling on television ownership was set at a 15 per cent share of UK audience time, with BBC audiences included for the purposes of calculating the total UK television audience.[8] The only remaining restrictions, alongside the 15 per cent of total audience share limit, apply to common ownership of certain terrestrial licences. These are that no single provider may own two ITV licences in the same area (i.e. both of the London ITV licences), and that no single provider may own both an ITV and a C5 licence. The ITC is empowered to revoke a television licence in circumstances where the 15 per cent upper audience limit is breached.

In addition, by way of mitigating possible adverse effects of consolidation of ownership within ITV, the 1996 Act includes more explicit measures than existed under the 1990 Act to protect the regional character of ITV.[9] The ITC is empowered to impose new conditions on an ITV licensee where it considers that a change of ownership may prejudice the quality of its programming or regional production.

The 1996 Act also introduced the general framework for digital broadcasting in the UK. As far as television ownership is concerned, there are no special restrictions on operating digital television multiplexes and any company may hold up to three television multiplex licences. Television companies are also free to own digital terrestrial television services, subject to the overall 15 per cent total television audience limit. Under the 1996 Act, ownership of digital services was also made subject to a separate points system whereby no single broadcaster could account for more than 25 per cent of digital terrestrial frequencies but the Secretary of State for Culture, Media and Sport abolished this rule by secondary legislation in November 2000.

The 1996 Act allows, for the first time, significant levels of cross-ownership between newspaper groups, radio stations and terrestrial television companies, at both the national and regional levels. Prior to 1996, newspaper groups, radio companies and terrestrial television broadcasters were only allowed to have minority investment stakes in each other's activities. The new Act swept away these restrictions and allows a single provider to own any combination of the following: up to 15 per cent of the radio sector (excluding BBC audiences) but no more than one national radio licence; plus up to 15 per cent of the television sector (including BBC audiences) but not more than one national ITV or C5 licence; plus up to 20 per cent of national daily newspaper circulations.

Notably, monomedia ownership of newspapers is not touched upon in the 1996 Act. The new 20 per cent upper ceiling on newspaper ownership comes into effect only in the case of cross-media expansion. In other words, ownership of more than 20 per cent of national daily newspaper circulations will only disallow a proprietor from cross-owning terrestrial television and/or commercial radio licences, and vice versa.[10] As was the case under the 1990 Act, cross-ownership restrictions do not apply between newspapers and cable or satellite broadcasters.

At the local or regional level, cross-ownership of terrestrial television and radio licences covering the same transmission areas remains prohibited but cross-ownership between local newspapers and broadcasters was substantially deregulated under the 1996 Act. Local newspaper proprietors may now own regional terrestrial television licences, although a circulation share of more than 20 per cent in the target's transmission area will prevent cross-ownership. Similarly, a market share in excess of 50 per cent of the target's transmission area will rule out cross-ownership of local radio services (and vice versa), unless at least one other such radio service is also operating in the same locality.

At the same time as allowing higher levels of cross-media ownership, the 1996 Act also introduces a new measure – the so-called 'public interest' test – which gives regulators discretionary power to block undesirable mergers if such action can be justified as being in the public interest.[11] In the case of any merger or takeover between newspaper proprietors and terrestrial television or radio broadcasters, whether at the national or regional level, the relevant broadcasting authority (i.e. either the ITC or the RA) is required to carry out a public interest test, taking into account plurality and diversity, any economic benefits arising from the deal, and its effect on the proper operation of the newspaper and broadcasting markets. The relevant authority will give its consent unless it finds reason to expect that a proposed takeover or merger would be likely to operate against the public interest.

The regulatory changes introduced by the 1996 Broadcasting Act represented a sweeping shift in UK media ownership policy. The restrictions which had prevailed, up until the 1994–95 review of cross-media ownership, were undoubtedly open to criticism, especially regarding their lack of effectiveness in curtailing the dominance of one particular media owner – News International (Hitchens, 1995). Yet, rather than opening up any possibility of strengthening safeguards for pluralism, the proposals offered by the 1994–95 Review Committee steered the redesign of policy inexorably in the opposite direction towards a widespread liberalization of media ownership.

The explanation for the relaxation of media and cross-media ownership rules appears to lie in the 'economic' arguments submitted to the DNH by many large UK media firms and, also, in the Government's receptiveness to these arguments. The following chapter examines more closely how the conflict between such pro-liberalization industrial arguments and concerns to preserve pluralism played itself out in the UK policy-making arena. What the UK experience demonstrates, above all else, is the crucial significance in the reshaping of rules on media ownership of underlying power relations between politicians and media owners.

## Notes

1. Section 59.

2. The facts underlying the case of the takeover of Times Newspapers by News International in 1981 are analysed in detail in Robertson and Nicol (1992: 503–5).

3. C5 was the (then) proposed fifth and final national terrestrial channel. The licence was subsequently awared to Channel 5 TV in April 1996.

4. The 1990 Broadcasting Act restricted ownership to no more than two C3 (ITV) licences and, in accompanying secondary legislation, a further stipulation prevented ownership of any more than one 'large' and one 'small' ITV regional licence. 'Small' licences were defined by the ITC as those attracting a share of less than 4 per cent of ITV's collective net advertising revenue (NAR).

5. Ownership of commercial radio is governed by a system whereby each licence is allocated points according to the size of the population served by that licence.

6. The Broadcasting (Restriction on Holding of Licences) (Amendment) Order 1995 (SI 1995/1924) came into force on 21 July 1995.

7. The Broadcasting (Independent Productions) (Amendment) Order 1995 (SI 1995/1925) also came into effect on 21 July 1995.

8. 1996 Broadcasting Act, para. 2, Part III, Schedule 2.

9. Contained in Sections 78 and 79 of the Act.

10. Para. 4, Part IV, Schedule 2 – This is the controversial clause which excludes both News International and Mirror Group Newspapers from expansion into terrestrial television.

11. Paras 9–13, Part IV, Schedule 2.

# 7

# The 1996 Broadcasting Act – An Analysis

The 1996 Broadcasting Act was, according to the Government, intended to 'liberate British broadcasters to be world leaders in the 21st century' (DNH, 1995c: 1). But, now that the 21st century has arrived, there is precious little sign of UK broadcasters competing more effectively than before in overseas markets. What, then, was the point of liberalizing UK media ownership policy? This chapter analyses the changes in monomedia and cross-media ownership rules brought about by the 1996 Act. Drawing on evidence concerning the economic performance of leading UK media firms discussed in Part II, and on findings from interviews carried out with senior UK policy-makers involved in 'shepherding through' the changes, this chapter assesses what, if any, benefits have stemmed from the new measures which the 1996 Act introduced.[1]

The key concerns and objectives which the new legislation was intended to address were outlined in the Green Paper, *Media Ownership*, of May 1995:

> Government has a responsibility both to promote *diversity* and choice for consumers and to set *the right framework for industry to flourish* . . . The main objective . . . [is] . . . to secure a plurality of sources of information and opinion, and a plurality of editorial control over them. Another important objective is to provide the environment to enable UK broadcasters, equipment manufacturers and programme makers to take full advantage of major market opportunities . . .
> . . . the existing structure of media ownership regulation, relying as it does on prohibitions which reinforce the traditional segmentation of the media market, is insufficiently flexible to allow media companies to exploit to the full the opportunities offered by new technologies . . .
> The Government has decided that there is a continuing case for specific regulations governing media ownership, beyond those which are applied by the general competition law; but that there is a need to liberalise the existing ownership regulations both within and across different media sectors. (DNH, 1995a: 16, 20, 1)

Although some amendments were introduced between the proposals set out in this Green Paper and the legislation finally enacted in 1996, the Government remained steadfast throughout the period in its espoused commitment to the two key priorities expressed above: promoting pluralism and accommodating the successful economic development of industry. The policy aims underlying these two key priorities may be categorized as those of a socio-political nature – i.e. promoting plurality (or avoiding excessive dominance by any individual 'voice' in the media); and those of an economic nature – i.e. preserving competition, promoting efficiency and encouraging the international competitiveness of UK media firms (or avoiding hindrances to the commercial success of industry).

The simultaneous pursuit of both of these broad objectives creates an obvious conflict – pluralism would require more effective restraints on ownership whereas industrial aspirations call for deregulation. Policy-makers at the Department of National Heritage were charged with reconciling these objectives within a single regulatory framework. As the evidence discussed below indicates, concerns about the Government's relationship with the press during the policy formulation period were uppermost in deciding how these conflicting aims were traded off against each other. Thus, the role played by wider political forces and by the conduct of the process of policy-making itself, as opposed to the pursuit of espoused policy aims, emerge as crucial issues in this assessment.

## Socio-political agenda

### Safeguarding pluralism

> The main objective . . . [of media ownership policy is] . . . to secure a plurality of sources of information and opinion, and a plurality of editorial control over them. (DNH, 1995a: 16)

At its most basic level, the 'pluralism' objective is about ensuring that the structure of media provision allows for a diversity of independent viewpoints – an open traffic in opinions, ideas or forms of cultural expression. Although safeguarding pluralism was presented as the main priority, the new media ownership provisions drafted by the DNH into the ensuing 1996 Broadcasting Act actually offer *less* rather than more protection of pluralism. Not only were monomedia ownership ceilings raised, especially in the case of terrestrial television, but previous restrictions on cross-media ownership between national newspapers proprietors and terrestrial television were largely done away with (although the two largest national newspaper owners, News International and Mirror Group Newspapers, are still prevented from expansion into terrestrial television). In effect, the new media ownership provisions allow for radio, television and newspapers in the UK to be supplied by fewer media owners than had previously, under the 1990 media ownership legislation, been considered an acceptable minimum. In practice, this has resulted in much greater concentration of ownership of UK terrestrial television and in some additional cross-ownership between newspaper and television providers.

According to policy-makers, the failure to try and turn what was presented as the main objective – pluralism – into more effective media ownership legislation is accounted for partly by prevailing perceptions that the general impetus for reviewing media ownership rules was a de-regulatory one. The industrial case in favour of liberalizing media ownership regulations was highly influential and, for the DNH, there appeared to be few persuasive proponents of the opposite case in favour of imposing more effective restrictions.

The irresistible logic, for MPs and policy-makers, of pro-liberalization arguments cannot be entirely dissociated from the immense power of the voices which conveyed this point of view. Whereas many large UK newspaper groups and other media owners favoured deregulation, the opposite side of the issue was primarily argued by individual trade unions, and a handful of consumer groups and academics. Policy-makers at the DNH acknowledge that those responsible for conducting the public debate about media ownership rule changes had a particular vested interest in its outcome; they were conscious that self-interested media owners had the capacity 'to create completely artificial currents of opinion'. The response chosen to deal with the power of media owners was the adoption of a 'tactical' approach. This approach was summarized by a DNH policy-maker as follows:

> Broadly speaking, what we did was say [to the media] 'Well look, we are not in a position to wholly jettison the other side of the argument. We are satisfied, within Government, following months and months of examination, that there are still these positive goods on the plurality and diversity side.'
>
> I think, to be honest, what was done was simply to calculate how much needed to be done in order to buy off most of the media and, in particular, the newspaper sector of the media, to the extent that they would say that they would back up our proposals and say that they were a good statesman-like thing. And that then, having sort of covered ourselves by going what we assessed as that far, or far enough in that direction, we could then (as indeed we *did* during the passage of the Bill) spend most of our time defending ourselves against attacks designed to engender yet further liberalization.

So, a tacit negotiation took place between the Government and the press which paved the way not only for 'most' media owners to gain exactly the de-regulatory concessions they were seeking but also, ironically, for the Government to present itself thereafter as a stout defender of the public interest in pluralism.

The danger that political factors may outweigh public interest considerations (of any kind) might be regarded as a general occupational hazard for regulation of the media. In this specific case of the reformulation of UK media ownership policy, it appears to have been a systemic failing of the process, in that it was not merely the Government of the day – i.e. Conservative MPs – who were muted in their support for more effective restraints on excessive media power, but opposition Labour MPs also. In fact, a Labour supported amendment which would have enacted an even more substantial liberalization of cross-media ownership was only narrowly resisted by the Government during the Commons Committee stage of the Broadcasting Bill in spring 1996.

The absence of an influential supporting constituency for pluralism meant that it – the so-called main objective for the new media ownership rules – became consigned to ministerial rhetoric rather than any meaningful priority for those drafting legislative changes. Pitched against the desires of a much more powerful sectional interest – media owners – the arguments of those defending the public interest in pluralism left virtually no impression on policy-making. A notable aspect of this situation is the failure, at every level, to take proper account of existing media power as a potential and actual obstruction to the development, in the first place, of any supporting constituency for pluralism. Notwithstanding the acknowledged role of a self-interested media in creating the prevailing climate of opinion, no special steps were taken to promote public awareness and discussion of the issues outside of the media.

Furthermore, to the extent that there existed any political will even to reflect upon pluralism and on the possible socio-political or cultural consequences of reducing media ownership restraints, it seems that little in the way of independent analysis was available for guidance. The absence of relevant information upon which to base policy decisions signals a notable lapse from what might be expected under rational policy-making conditions (Hogwood and Gunn, 1984: 45). DNH policy-makers apparently relied instead on their 'intuitions' about what levels of media and cross-media concentration of ownership would seem acceptable.

In short, the redesign of UK media ownership policy was characterized from beginning to end by lack of proper information gathering or analysis. Of particular concern is the fact that securing the approval of most media owners for where the new media and cross-media ownership levels would be set – or 'getting the BMIG on-side' – was clearly regarded as the key imperative. This explains how pluralism slipped from the high status accorded to it in the policy agenda presented by Government to the public. Of greater significance, perhaps, is what it appears to suggest about how policies involving the media take shape in the UK.

Existing levels of political influence on the part of UK media owners are such that media policies appear to be predicated largely on industry's requirements rather than on the best interests of the consumer or society at large. In purporting to be democratic, the UK system of political decision-making implies uppermost concern with the latter – the interests and wishes of 'the people' (Smith, 1976: 28). So the situation exemplified by revisions of UK media ownership in the 1996 Broadcasting Act underlines concerns previously raised by scholars such as Lasswell and Lindblom, about the impact on democracy of 'the interests and manipulations of powerful elites' (Parsons, 1995: 614). As noted by many other theorists concerned with the role of the media in politics, democracy is particularly threatened when self-interested elites have the capacity to set policy agendas and manipulate public opinion (1995: 106–45).

From the point of view of society, the main concern may not be the many individual instances of monomedia, vertical or diagonal expansion by UK media companies which have followed on from the 1996 Act. The strengthening of an indigenous media supplier in Scotland, for example, certainly has its attractions from a socio-cultural point of view. Taken as a whole, however, what these corporate changes represent is the reinforcement of political power for a commercial sector which shows no hesitation in using this power to promote its own interests, irrespective of other societal concerns. It would, perhaps, be unreasonable to expect a commercial sector which is empowered to influence its own regulatory environment to pursue any interest other than its own. A major concern for society is that if the need to 'buy off' the media predominates over the design of public policy in one area, it cannot be assumed that such a need would not impose itself in other areas, even where the interests of media owners are not visibly at stake.

## Securing effective and equitable constraints

> If one voice becomes too strong ... democracy is damaged. (DNH, 1995a: 3)

Part of protecting the public interest in diverse media ownership is the duty, acknowledged in the 1995 Green Paper, to place equal restraints on *all* media owners and to prevent any single individual or organization from gaining too much influence over public opinion. But another questionable feature of the 1996 legislation is that it perpetuates long-standing failures to bring about any such equitable constraints on the upper share of media power that anyone may have. As one UK national newspaper manager points out: 'there is a [public interest] case to say you don't want one person owning all newspapers. Funnily enough, the 1996 Broadcasting Act does not stop that. You just can't *cross*-own.' The 1996 Act established upper ceilings on cross-media ownership, and on monomedia ownership within the television and the radio sectors. But, it said nothing about monomedia ownership of newspapers. Thus, a situation was allowed to continue where some 38 per cent of national daily newspaper circulation in the UK is controlled by just one owner – News International.

DNH policy-makers account for this gap by explaining that they were placed in the position of enacting the wishes of ministers. Despite widespread recognition of the benefits enjoyed by one company in particular because of the scale and diversity of its media interests in the UK, there was little or no will to place upper ceilings on newspaper ownership. Many felt that, rather than imposing new controls on News International, a better solution would be to strengthen the position of competitors. The prevailing perception was, quite unambiguously, that the general thrust of new measures ought to be deregulatory rather than introducing new restraints. The main beneficiary of this approach was the highly influential lobby group, BMIG.

The extent to which the 1995 Green Paper and the 1996 Act reflect ideas favoured by the BMIG (BMIG, 1994, 1995) seems clearly indicative of policy-making as a 'selective response' to institutional interests (Levin, 1997: 38–41). Cross-ownership between national newspapers and terrestrial television was liberalised, but only for those newspaper proprietors with a share of national circulations of less than 20 per cent. This 20 per cent upper ceiling on cross-media expansion by newspaper proprietors enabled all members of the BMIG to move into terrestrial television. According to the Corporate Strategy Director of a major UK publishing and broadcasting company:

> The liberalization in the 1996 Act was largely driven by [Newspaper Group A, B and C] . . . They had a huge influence on that whole process and were successful. The way Westminster works is so sleazy and the next lot won't be any better – the only chance is Parliamentary reform . . .
>
> Those guys [Newspaper Group A, B and C] were big opinion formers – one the editor of a national mass-market daily. As media owners at the national level, their access to politicians, not just Tory politicians but *all* politicians, is incredibly good.

If the relaxation of cross-ownership limits between newspapers, television and radio in the 1996 Act suited 'most' media industry participants, it was not received with equal enthusiasm by the two newspaper groups prevented from expansion into terrestrial television. Many people, even within the BMIG, were conscious that in seeking to exert some constraint on the expansion of the man who is perceived as the most powerful media baron in the UK – Rupert Murdoch – the simultaneous impact of the 20 per cent cross-ownership ceiling in constraining one other smaller media company (with Labour sympathies) – Mirror Group Newspapers – was likely to be unpopular in some quarters. One former member of the BMIG acknowledged the position at the Mirror Group thus:

> It is interesting that the Labour Party has a different view on this. I could understand Mirror Group's frustration – they are much smaller than News International. David Montgomery was outraged . . . justifiably so.

The imposition of cross-media newspaper ownership limits which prevent the two largest UK newspaper groups from expanding into terrestrial TV can certainly be seen as defending the public interest in pluralism. But it is not the same thing as insisting that all newspaper proprietors be brought back within sensible or reasonable common upper levels of newspaper ownership. Apparently, existing excesses of media power provide the context in which few if any politicians were prepared to contemplate proposing such curbs, irrespective of the public interest.

The reformulation of media ownership rules in the UK seems to exemplify both the strength and the importance of the relationship between politicians and the press, yet understandably, as noted by the Finance Director of a major UK media firm, there is a general reluctance to draw this issue into the public domain:

> There is a very big national interest in the relationship between Government and the media, but there is also a political dimension to it all. Whether it was [title X] that won the election for the Conservatives the last time or whether it will be [title X] that wins it for Labour this time you can discuss . . . But it means that you may not get very open discussion about it, either from the politicians or maybe from the media.

Another striking anomaly is that monomedia ownership restrictions – acceptable upper audience limits for television and for radio – were set at completely different levels in the 1996 Act, with commercial television operators effectively allowed to have a market share twice as large as commercial radio operators. Whereas television ownership is restricted to a 15 per cent share of total UK audiences *including* BBC audiences, radio ownership remains restricted to a 15 per cent share of total UK audiences *excluding* BBC audiences. Given that the BBC enjoys a share of almost one half of total UK audiences both in television and in radio, the decision about whether to include or exclude those audiences when computing any other individual organization's market share is of immense significance. The effect of including BBC audiences within the total television market is to almost double the size of that market and thus to double the audience share a commercial television broadcaster may serve, in comparison with what is allowed for commercial radio broadcasters.

Most people would regard television as a more powerful medium than radio. So there does not seem to be any logical justification for imposing a tighter check on ownership of commercial radio than on ownership of commercial television broadcasting licences. Many industry players acknowledge that inconsistencies of this sort in the regulation of media ownership are primarily a reflection of different levels of political clout on the part of media owners. One corporate strategist observed that:

> Newspapers were the main protagonists lobbying for relaxation . . . whereas the radio industry represent itself less effectively. Plus there were TV players lobbying as well and clearly their agenda was to consolidate the C3 [ITV] network, and that is exactly what they've done . . . 15 per cent [of television audiences] sounds very innocuous but, in terms of the commercial TV market, it is almost a 30 per cent share.

Whatever intentions were expressed to produce a system of media ownership controls in the UK which would prevent any single voice from becoming too strong, it is difficult to escape the conclusion that this problem already existed. Because the voices of certain media owners were already too powerful to allow policy-makers to adopt a truly even-handed approach, the new provisions set out in the 1996 Broadcasting Act are awash with inconsistencies which have only served to reinforce the problem.

## Economic agenda

> Government has a responsibility . . . to set the right framework for the industry to flourish. (DNH, 1995a: 16)

### Competition in domestic media markets

As discussed in Chapter 3, one aspect of the Government's responsibility for setting the right economic framework for the development of the media sector is to create the circumstances in which competition will flourish and take place on a fair and equal basis. In the media, as in all other sectors of industry, instances of anti-competitive behaviour tend to fall under the jurisdiction of competition law; competition issues such as, for example, predatory pricing are not generally seen as a specific concern for media ownership regulation. Whereas special media ownership restrictions (based primarily on the need for pluralism) provide a supplement to competition rules, they do not replace the need for competition legislation or for the competition authorities to investigate and deal with instances of restrictive or anti-competitive behaviour involving media companies.

Indeed, the prevalence of highly concentrated ownership levels both within and across some sectors of the UK media (despite the safeguards provided by special restrictions on media ownership) has led to many allegations of anti-competitive behaviour that have had to be considered and dealt with under competition rules. Even so, because both media ownership rules and competition rules are broadly concerned with preventing media owners from abusing their market positions (albeit on account of quite different underlying concerns), there is a tendency amongst some industry participants to regard them as carrying out much the same function.

Rather than viewing specific media ownership rules as a useful complementary tier of legislation which protects pluralism, some would rather see these done away with altogether in favour of a regulatory regime based solely on competition considerations. According to the Chief Executive of a major newspaper publishing company:

> There is no need for most of the [UK media ownership] rules. I assume that they're to stop dominance but they're based on politicians' paranoia . . . politicians always believe that you should publish what they want to read about themselves, and not what they don't want. Politicians are the worst people to regulate the media because they have a vested interest.
>
> I think that normal monopoly rules should apply to the media. There should not be any rules over and above that. And they have to dismantle regulation through organizations like the ITC because it's like living in a nanny state . . .

While many commercial media operators are sceptical about the need for virtually any special regulatory constraints over their activities, some acknowledge that competition rules may not be an entirely effective way of constraining the power of media moguls. Another UK newspaper executive points out that the problem with using competition law and relying merely on its approach of carrying out a public interest test is that judgements 'depend on the Government of the day and how they are advised'. Competition rules and the case-by-case approach are less likely to achieve consistency and equality than clearly drawn media and cross-media ownership limits.

Although media ownership legislation is not designed or intended to deal specifically with issues of unfair competition between rival media suppliers, the competition regime and potential for abuses of market power which have resulted from excessive concentrations of media ownership in the UK have created a critical view of media ownership law. But criticisms that ownership rules in the 1996 Broadcasting Act UK have failed to tackle competition effectively are, in a sense, misdirected. The 1995 Green Paper on media ownership clearly indicated that the potential for anti-competitive behaviour (for example, by gatekeeper monopolists in broadcasting) is an issue to do with 'the proper operation of the market' (DNH, 1995a: 18) and is therefore subject to general competition law rather than media ownership policy.

Such criticisms are, however, understandable. If dominant media owners in the UK are able to abuse their market position, this implies the need for tighter controls over their market share. A confusion about roles and responsibilities is not surprising given that, in addition to distorting competition, any instance of abuse of market power (for example deterring or denying market access to potential rivals) would also have a detrimental effect on media diversity, which *is* the concern of media ownership regulation. So, perceptions that the 1996 Act ought to have done more to promote competition and sustain market access (for example in the pay-television sector) are not without some validity.

## Promoting economic efficiency

The most important consideration guiding the reformulation of media ownership rules in the 1996 Act seems to have been creating the conditions for industry to 'flourish', i.e. establishing a framework which would strengthen the economic performance of the UK media industry. As discussed in Chapter 6, many large media industry participants had called for a general liberalization of previous media ownership rules, based on the argument that this would enable greater efficiency and thus improved economic performance by the sector.

To assess the likely economic impact of the 1996 media ownership legislation changes, it is helpful to consider the relationship between *allowable* and *economically desirable* configurations for media firms. In order to fully exploit economies of scale and scope in the media, certain configurations are more desirable than others. Media ownership legislation in the UK, before and after the 1996 Broadcasting Act, places no constraints on very many potential configurations of media enterprise; it has only ever affected levels of monomedia and cross-media ownership involving radio, television and newspapers.

The main impact of rule changes in the 1996 Act is to allow, for the first time, significant levels of cross-ownership of television, radio and newspapers and also to allow much higher levels of (terrestrial) television ownership than before. This has enabled new configurations to flourish, but not all such configurations are 'desirable' on the grounds of improved economic efficiency. According to the evidence considered in Part II above, the only change from previous restrictions which is unambiguously supported by the potential for additional economic efficiency gains is the relaxation of monomedia restrictions affecting the traditional sectors of the media. There is little or no economic evidence to support a case for liberalizing cross-media restrictions affecting television, radio and newspapers. This is because, on the whole, the economic performance of television, radio and newspaper firms does point to clearly identifiable benefits arising from expansion *within* each of these individual sectors of activity. On the other hand, diagonal cross-media expansion *across*, say, newspapers and television appears *not* to be well-supported by any specific economies of scope or inherent cross-synergies.

The common upper ceiling, for all UK television companies, of 15 per cent of the total UK television audience paved the way for much additional consolidation of ownership within the commercial television sector (e.g. Carlton TV's takeover of Westcountry TV in December 1996 and Scottish Television's takeover of Grampian Television in 1997). According to evidence provided by many leading UK television companies, such consolidation yields various opportunities for broadcasters to consolidate back-office functions such as finance and administration and it creates opportunities to derive collective cost-savings on specialist activities such as transmission and airtime sales. According to the Finance Director of a large ITV company:

> The media ownership rules prior to 1996 imposed constraints ... on all the ITV companies because you couldn't have more than two licences ...
>
> The trouble is that ITV's federal structure is incredibly debilitating, and the new rules go some way to correcting that ...
>
> I think the new 15 per cent ceiling on TV ownership is about right but I'm sure they'll want to revisit it in 2–3 years' time, because it's such a fast-changing environment.

The potential for gaining additional cost-efficiencies through consolidation within ITV is, to some extent at least, limited by the obligation under the 1996 Act for all licensees to maintain regional programming activities and investment in associated resources, irrespective of any ownership changes. It is also limited by the fact that each regional ITV licensee already participates in a variety of collective cost-sharing arrangements (e.g. on network programming, transmission and airtime sales) which, in large measure, cannot be streamlined any further. Nonetheless, some significant additional cost-savings are only possible through further consolidation and – provided that there is no detrimental impact on the quality of programming output – the achievement of these savings represents a benefit. The removal of waste – i.e. unnecessary duplication of resources – within the television industry is, undeniably, a desirable economic outcome (Martin, 1993: 266).

So, as discussed in Chapter 4, monomedia expansion within the television industry may give rise to organizational configurations which are more economically efficient. Indeed, the same can be said for expansion within the radio broadcasting sector or within the newspaper publishing industry. For each of these activities, the prevalence of economies of scale and scope will inevitably tend to favour the economic performance of firms that command a larger share of the market.

But what about *cross*-media mergers? Very many combinations of cross-media ownership evidently *do* also give rise to synergies and other positive economic benefits for diversified media enterprises such as Pearson. The combinations of cross-ownership that yield the most significant efficiency gains are those that allow either specialized content or a distribution infrastructure to be shared across different sectors or product markets. However, there is little compelling evidence to suggest that increased cross-ownership between *television and newspaper* operators – the other key deregulatory concession afforded in the 1996 Act – would give rise to any economic benefits. An analysis of historic trading figures provides no indication that those UK media firms involved both in television broadcasting and in newspaper publishing have achieved higher operating profitability than rivals engaged in only one of these activities. In addition, few senior UK media managers seem convinced that there are any real operational synergies between television broadcasting and newspaper publishing.

This brings to light an important discrepancy. According to the arguments in favour of deregulation set out in the 1995 Green Paper, the availability of cross-synergies between newspapers and broadcasters represented a definite and major impetus for relaxing previous restraints on cross-media ownership. Yet several senior managers in the UK newspaper and broadcasting industries have strong doubts about whether television broadcasting and newspaper publishing offer any substantive synergies. Most agree that the skills involved in newspaper publishing are really quite *different* from those required in the television industry, and vice versa. As one Director of Corporate Affairs put it: 'There is *not* a lot of cross-over in editorial, production or distribution techniques between TV and newspapers . . . [although] there was a lot of hype about cross-synergies.'

The economic rationale for bringing together newspaper and television operations within a single organization seems quite limited. The most important special advantage of cross-owning television and newspapers appears to be the opportunity to cross-promote products. But the broader economic implications of this are questionable. Cross-promotion used to launch new products that widen choice is likely to benefit consumers. But if cross-promotion merely serves to strengthen the dominance of existing products and players then competition and pluralism will be damaged.

When questioned on this, a senior DNH policy-makers readily acknowledged the dearth of persuasive evidence to support the view that combined television-newspaper ownership is an economically desirable configuration:

> At various points the newspaper industry argued that there were cross-synergies, but the television side always denied that this could ever be the case. The basis of news reporting for newspapers was entirely different from that in news reporting for television. You'd never get common news outfits to be able to deal both with printed or spoken and visual images. So, I'm surprised if that was thought to be a major part in the argument . . .

But the reason why cross-synergies might be perceived as a major impetus for de-regulating cross-ownership in the 1996 Act is because this is the key argument in favour of deregulation which is set out in the 1995 Green Paper on media ownership:

> The Government believes that it is essential that the media ownership regime should allow the media sector to develop. The similarity of functions which newspapers and broadcasters undertake in terms of collecting, editing and disseminating information, news and entertainment, means that there are obvious and natural synergies between companies within each sector, and that it is the interests of both the industry and the consumer to allow larger media companies to develop. (DNH, 1995a: 20)

If, in fact, the Government and its advisors were deeply sceptical about the existence of 'obvious and natural synergies between companies within each sector', they nonetheless chose to adopt the arguments put forward by the newspaper industry in favour of de-regulating cross-ownership between the newspaper and television industry. A member of the DNH-led Review Committee on Cross-Media Ownership explains:

> What can I say? These were *political* decisions at root. Where it was convenient to try and have a veneer of an economic case, that case was deployed. But I certainly wouldn't want to leave the impression that it was economic arguments, rigorously constructed, that determined policy.

Even if ministers or policy-makers *had* wished to go beyond the 'clearly self-interested' submissions of industry participants in order to establish what the economic implications might be of amending UK media owner-ship legislation as certain industry groups saw fit, it would have been very difficult for them to do so. No research was available, nor was any commissioned, which would provide an independent assessment of either the economic or any other implications of altering the rules.

DNH policy-makers attribute this failing to 'the time-scale involved', to the fact that ministers were 'not interested' in independent research, and to the 'political minefield' that they were operating in during the passage of the 1995 Broadcasting Bill. But, as a possibility at least in this case, a more compelling explanation for formulating policy without recourse to appropriate information gathering and analysis could be the desire to avoid acknowledging falsehoods or illogicalities in the 'economic' argument used to support the preferred course of action (Carley, 1983: 33; Levin, 1997: 35). Any inconsistency between the findings of independent research and the economic rationale adopted by Government in favour of deregulating media cross-ownership would have been embarrassing and inconvenient.

If operational cross-synergies are not a strong feature of the newspaper and television industries, what explanation can there be for the pressure mounted by media firms in favour of a liberalization of cross-ownership rules? It is widely acknowledged that the main intention behind industrial lobbying was to clear the way for newspaper owners to diversify from their own relatively stagnant sector into the more profitable and promising growth areas in the media, such as terrestrial television. Of course, this argument in favour of allowing cross-ownership has no basis whatsoever in terms of improved operational or economic efficiency. Instead, it is based on securing a low-risk route to long-term earnings growth for incumbent newspaper proprietors and shareholders. But 'the veneer of an economic case' provided by convergence undoubtedly qualifies as a more respectable goal for public policy than the wish to accommodate the self-interest of newspaper owners.

The desire of many media firms to see cross-ownership restrictions removed via the 1996 Broadcasting Act can be explained by a range of self-interested motives. But the fact remains that the 'obvious and natural' cross-synergies between newspaper publishing and broadcasting referred to in the 1995 Green Paper are virtually non-existent. No visible economic benefits have resulted from the deregulation of cross-media ownership restraints between television broadcasting and newspapers.

### Encouraging international competitiveness

> Our proposals will liberate British broadcasters to become world leaders. (DNH, 1995c: 2)

Economic efficiency was not the only argument in favour of allowing larger media enterprises to develop. One of the key factors cited as lending weight to the case in favour of liberalization was the need to help UK media organizations compete more effectively in overseas markets.

The Green Paper on media ownership suggested, without explaining how, that liberalizing domestic UK cross-media ownership rules would benefit the performance of UK media firms in overseas markets (DNH, 1995a: 20). But none of the managers interviewed at leading UK media firms expected their export performance to be affected by provisions in the 1996 Act and most seemed bemused by the suggestion of a link between domestic ownership rule changes and likely exports performance. In spite of globalization, most UK media firms appear to be closely focused on the domestic UK market and show little sign of altering their outlook on account of the 1996 Act. As one Corporate Strategist explains:

> While bigger media companies may enjoy higher profits in the UK because they are larger and more efficient, it doesn't actually help them in terms of exports because this is not really a global market at the moment . . .
>
> That sort of speak (the need to create globally competitive players) was at the heart of competition policy in the 1980s. The same thing was said for airlines and then for telecoms . . . it's all about backing national players which could become competitive globally . . . backing winners. It works better in airlines and telecoms where regulations have fallen away in other countries as well *and* where it is truly a global market with a global customer base and real international transactions. But it's not like that for TV or newspapers. TV is obviously a local thing . . . it is amazing how badly and how little television content travels. Everyone thinks BBC quality drama and ITV output does well overseas but what sells is only a fraction of their programme budgets . . . The same goes for newspapers.

But even if liberalizing media ownership rules has had no immediate impact on the export performance of domestic media suppliers, it could indirectly contribute to the expansion of these firms into overseas markets. It can be argued that the range of corporate strategies and opportunities open to individual firms is affected, at least to some extent, by the scale of their existing resources (George et al., 1992: 101). Many industry participants agree that because larger companies tend to have more capital for investment in new areas, it follows that larger media companies have greater potential for international growth. The Finance Director of one of the UK's largest diversified media firms sums up the argument thus:

> You can't sell more programmes overseas because you own a newspaper, and I wouldn't claim that . . . It's just that larger scale helps; if you are bigger and stronger you can invest more.

Others, however, take the view that it is not necessarily the scale of existing resources that counts for media companies when it comes to expansion into new product or geographic markets. According to some, the main opportunities for international expansion are centred on newly emerging communication infrastructures such as the Internet rather than 'traditional' media products. The propensity to take risks may be a *more* crucial determinant of success than the size of the company. One Corporate Planner argues that big companies are not as inventive and innovative as their smaller rivals and that enlargement can actually impede firms from responding quickly to new opportunities:

> Of course, larger integrated media companies, in theory, have the resources and inclination to invest in developing these new opportunities. But few of them are actually doing so . . .
>   New media is not about a lot of money. The most successful companies have been built on very little – for example Reuters or BSkyB or Microsoft or Netscape. Having the size may give you the resources but it does not necessarily give you the vision and the mindset and the environment in which people will think creatively.

If, as now appears to be the case, the media ownership rule changes in the 1996 Act have had little or no impact on the international performance of UK media suppliers, it may well be because, in reality, the reshaping of these rules was a response to domestic political imperatives rather than to any persuasive vision of how best to promote the economic welfare of the UK media sector.

## The unstated agenda

> It would be idle to pretend that we instituted properly rigorous scientific/ economic analysis specifically to buttress our policy conclusions . . . This is too *political* a market to regulate primarily because of economic objectives.

This observation, from a DNH policy-maker closely involved in the media ownership policy changes set out in the 1996 Act, points to an apparent flaw in the mechanism by which media concentrations are supposed to be regulated. Links between the machinery of Government and the wider political system, of which the media represent a crucial component, are inescapable. Because politicians want to, or increasingly feel they need to, accommodate the needs of particular and influential media groups, there seems little will on their part to champion or even to investigate competing public interest goals associated with media ownership policy.

The problem of unhealthy alignments between corporate media power and political power is not confined to the UK. Humphreys has described the deregulation of media ownership in Germany and Italy, as well as the UK, as 'classic illustrations of the degree of political power exercised by powerful media corporations in capitalist democracies' (1997: 9). His suggestion that 'the main determinant of media policy in the 1990s seems to be policy makers' perception of what is in the economic interest' and that 'the "economic interest" conforms with the said corporations' interests' (1997: 19) is reinforced by the evidence discussed here.

It is, however, crucially important to distinguish between corporate aspirations and wider economic objectives. Policy measures which advance the commercial interests of particular media firms cannot be equated with, and should not be confused with, measures likely to enhance the general economic efficiency of industry.

The suggestion that 'the main determinant of media policy in the 1990s *seems to be* policy makers' perception of what is in the economic interest' (ibid.; my emphasis) is correct. However, the research findings reported here indicate that policy-makers' *real* beliefs about what is in the economic interest may differ significantly from what they choose or feel required to present to the public as their perception on this matter. The account presented to the public legitimizes, on economic grounds, the case for given policy recommendations. That account may well be based on a largely fictitious interpretation of economic realities but, nonetheless, such legitimization is needed to deflect attention from the fact that policy recommendations have been formulated in accordance with what is in the political interest.

The process by which UK policy on media ownership was re-formulated in the 1990s has previously been criticized for lacking rationality (Hitchens, 1995). Such criticism appears to be well deserved – the process evidently suffered from a variety of shortcomings, including lack of proper informa-tion gathering. 'Comprehensive rationality' is, of course, a somewhat idealistic model and might even be regarded as too 'unrealistic or impracticable' for the real world of public policy-making (Hogwood and

Gunn, 1984: 47). Even so, virtually all approaches to policy analysis stress the fundamental importance of collecting information and gathering knowledge (Parsons, 1995: 427–8). In theory, an inverse relationship exists between the extent to which the techniques deployed in policy determination involve information seeking and rational analysis and, on the other hand, the ability of powerful interest groups to predominate in decision-making (1995: 253–4). In practice, the case of media ownership policy-making in the UK provides an excellent working example of this relationship. Little information gathering and analysis was carried out and powerful corporate media interests triumphed in impressing their wishes onto the design of policy changes.

The extent to which experiences at the DNH typify the circumstances and conduct of media policy-making more generally is unclear. But one safe conclusion that emerges is that the policy-making mechanism in the UK which is supposed to safeguard democracy by curbing the political influence of media owners is not working properly. Excesses of media power already exist in the UK to the extent that any curbs on it have to first to be negotiated with the industry. The 1996 Broadcasting Act included a number of deregulatory concessions intended to 'buy off' the majority of media owners so that some relatively weak safeguards for pluralism could be sustained.

---

## Notes

1. Based on findings from interviews carried out in spring 1997 with senior civil servants at the Department of National Heritage (DNH) and also with managers at each of the media firms mentioned in Figure 4.1 (see p. 46). For reasons of confidentiality, interviewees are not individually named.

# 8

# A New Future for Communications?

To judge by the proposals set out in the White Paper on communications of December 2000, there is precious little that is 'new' about the latest approach towards regulation of media ownership in the UK. The White Paper – entitled *A New Future for Communications* – asserts that the Government is 'committed to reforming the rules which protect media plurality, in the light of the new converging market conditions' (DTI/DCMS, 2000: 4). The importance of access to a diversity of services is emphasized but, in a rather contrary vein, rules governing diversity of monomedia ownership are to be relaxed. The White Paper suggests that existing upper limits on television and radio ownership are outdated and need to be replaced in a forthcoming Communications Act intended 'to maintain the UK's competitive advantage in the rapidly changing international marketplace' (2000: 3). In addition, views are called for on whether or not to liberalise cross-ownership restrictions affecting the UK's largest newspaper proprietors.

Evidence of a continuing wish to accommodate strategies of industrial concentration by relaxing or else removing media ownership rules may disappoint those who hoped that a change of Government at the 1997 general election in the UK would bring about a more energetic approach towards curbing media empires. But, for New Labour just as for the previous Conservative administration, pluralism seems to be consigned to the back burner while the real priority driving media ownership policy changes is a desire to facilitate the ambitions and concerns of major UK commercial media players. A further continuation along the deregulatory course first embarked upon a decade earlier will not surprise some sceptics in industry. As one media executive (cited earlier) observed in relation to the role played by the BMIG in determining media ownership policy changes in the 1990s: 'They had a huge influence on that whole process and were successful. The way Westminster works is so sleazy and the next lot won't be any better . . .'

The proposals set out in the communications White Paper of 2000 suggest that, after a period of only four years, the restrictions on ownership contained in the 1996 Broadcasting Act are already out of date. The decision to take action in 'reforming' legislation comes against a background of almost continuous corporate activity across the media and communications industries both in the UK and internationally. Mergers, acquisitions and other alliances involving television companies, newspaper groups, publishers, telecommunications operators, content creators or Internet-based media providers were rarely out of the headlines of the financial press in the late 1990s.

The scale of mergers involving media and communications firms at the international level has, in some cases, been dramatic. For example, the merger between US telecommunications operator AT&T and cable television giant TCI announced in 1998 created an enterprise valued at some $48 billion. In Europe, the acquisition of Dutch programme producer Endemol by Spanish telecoms operator Telefónica in 2000 provided another example of a major link-up between content creation and distribution. But the deal that has undoubtedly attracted more attention than any other in recent years was the high-profile $164 billion acquisition of US media conglomerate Time Warner by Internet service provider America Online which was announced in January 2000.

The emergence of global giants such as AOL/Time Warner has tended to fuel perceptions that UK players are at a disadvantage compared with large, diversified multinational rivals. As noted by Hughes, '[t]he UK market valuations of all companies populating the publishing, audiovisual, IT and telephony sectors amounts to $840bn, which is less than the market capitalisation of the two largest [communications] companies in America, Cisco and Microsoft'(2000: 25). UK firms such as, for example, Scottish Media Group take the view that further deregulation of media ownership is required to enable domestic companies 'to achieve the necessary scale to invest in products and services to compete with large international groups' (SMG, 2001: 6).

Some UK firms have made strenuous efforts to match the scale of leading media players in other countries, notwithstanding domestic regulatory constraints. A series of corporate manoeuvres involving ambitious ITV companies such as Carlton, SMG and Granada Media took place in the late 1990s. In 2000, a merger involving the television interests of UK media conglomerate Pearson and those of Audiofina of Belgium and Germany's Bertelsmann created a very substantial new pan-European television enterprise. Also in 2000, UK programme producer Flextech merged with cable operator TeleWest.

But the development which has probably been most significant in placing media ownership back onto the UK policy agenda has been consolidation of ownership within ITV. As discussed earlier, ITV is a network comprised of 14 separate regional broadcasting licences, several of which are now held in common ownership by a handful of large television companies. The first wave of ITV takeovers took place almost before the ink had time to dry on the 1996 Broadcasting Act. Carlton (owner of the London weekday and Central England ITV regional licences) acquired Westcountry (which ran the licence covering the South-West of England) in December 1996. Earlier in 1996, United Newspapers had merged with MAI (owner of South-East and East of England licences) to become United News & Media (UN&M) and, in 1997, the enlarged group acquired HTV (operator of the ITV licence for Wales and the West). Also in 1997, Scottish Media Group (owner of the Central Scotland licence) acquired Grampian (which operated the North of Scotland licence). In the same year, Granada (owner of licences for North-West and London weekend) acquired Yorkshire Tyne-Tees (which operated licences covering Yorkshire and the North-East of England). Two of the smallest companies in the ITV network – Ulster TV and Border – were the only ones to be overlooked in the consolidation process.

This initial flurry of corporate activity resulted in three major ITV players – Carlton, Granada and UN&M – plus, in Scotland, Scottish Media Group. Although none of the three major players had yet reached the upper ceiling for television ownership set at 15 per cent of total UK audience time in the 1996 Act, any further merger activity involving these companies might have led to this limit being overstepped. And a further less formal constraint on multiple ownership of ITV licenses existed in the form of an undertaking given by the ITV companies to the Office of Fair Trading in 1994 that no single company would acquire a share of UK television net advertising revenue of more than 25 per cent. This upper limit on any company's share of NAR was a secondary measure intended to preserve competition in advertising sales and to prevent abusive behaviour (in particular, overcharging) in markets for UK television airtime. Any further concentration of ITV ownership in the late 1990s was liable to result in a breach of this 25 per cent NAR limit.

However, further pressures to consolidate existed within ITV and it appeared that the scene was set to accommodate such consolidation when, in a speech given to the Royal Television Society in September 1999, the Minister for Culture, Media and Sport referred to the role of the Government in 'removing barriers to investment and expansion' in the broadcasting industry. Chris Smith noted various changes sweeping across the industry and reflected on a future in which broadcasting regulation would be 'based, in the first instance, on competition law with a reduced set of distinctive media rules added only where strictly necessary'.[1] This landmark speech made it abundantly clear which direction Government policy on regulation of broadcasting and, especially, on broadcasting ownership would be heading in the 21st century.

Shortly afterwards, at the end of November 1999, Carlton Communications and United News & Media announced plans to merge their media operations in a move which would reduce the number of major ITV players from three to two and give Carlton/UN&M a substantial lead over Granada. This proposed merger would result in a company with a combined television audience share of some 14.8 per cent which, importantly, meant that the deal was not in breach of the 15 per cent upper share of audience limit set out in the 1996 Broadcasting Act. But the agreed merger would give the enlarged company a combined share of UK television advertising of some 36 per cent, which was well in excess of the 25 per cent upper NAR limit agreed between ITV and the OFT back in 1994. If the merger was to proceed, Carlton and United News & Media would need to persuade the OFT to relax this 25 per cent limit.

A new complication arose however when, a few weeks after the Carlton/UN&M merger announcement, Granada asked the OFT to register its interest in acquiring either Carlton or United News & Media. Granada had an audience share of some 10.6 per cent in January 2000 (compared with 8.3 per cent for Carlton and 6.5 per cent for UN&M), which meant that either of its proposed bids would result in a single company with a combined television audience share of more than 15 per cent (see Table 8.1, p. 128). So, any move by Granada would have required the obligatory disposal of some of its television interests to comply with primary legislation.

Granada's announcement that it was interested in bidding for either Carlton or United News & Media acted as a signal that it was not willing to relinquish its dominant position within the ITV network without a fight (Larsen and O'Connor, 2000a: 16). Its intervention also proved successful as a 'spoiling tactic' in that it helped ensure that the proposed Carlton/UN&M deal was referred to the competition authorities for further investigation. In addition, Granada's expression of interest in bidding for one or other of its two main rivals meant that it gave itself the opportunity to become involved in that investigation and, as it subsequently transpired, to exert considerable influence over its outcome.

## Competition report on ITV mergers, 2000

The proposed merger of Carlton and United News & Media, and between Granada and either Carlton or United News & Media, were duly referred to the Competition Commission (CC) by the Secretary of State for Trade and Industry in February 2000. Some five months later, the Commission delivered its verdict in a lengthy report. The CC Report of July 2000 cleared both of the proposed mergers involving Granada (after taking account of obligatory divestments) but found that the agreed merger of Carlton and United News & Media 'could be expected to be contrary to the public interest' (CC, 2000: 5).

According to some, 'the most striking factor about the Commission's report – which was accepted fully by Stephen Byers, the Trade and Industry secretary – is the extent to which it accepts Granada's arguments and rejects those of its opponents' (Larsen and O'Connor, 2000b: 16). Others observed that '[t]he report reads very nearly like Granada's own submission to the Commission, accepting virtually every argument put forward by the owner of LWT, Yorkshire-Tyne Tees and Granada Television' (Horsman, 2000: 3). The Commission's findings, while obstructing the agreed merger between Carlton and UN&M, offered Granada the possibility of extending its portfolio of ownership within ITV through either of the acquisitions it wished to pursue.

The main concerns that the Commission addressed in its investigation were the possible effects of the proposed mergers on competition within airtime sales and on competition to supply programmes to the ITV network. Looking first at programming, the main worry for the Commission was that, because all three companies were already, to a greater or lesser extent, important suppliers of programmes to the ITV network, any further consolidation of ownership might result in excessive market dominance with possible anti-competitive effects. The position of 'independent' producers might be jeopardized, thus leading to a deterioration in programme quality.

Granada is by far the largest programme provider to ITV, supplying around 47 per cent of the network's original programme material in 1999 (CC, 2000: 105). This compares with a combined market share for Carlton and United News & Media of only 17.5 per cent in the same year. So, the most obvious concern was that any strengthening of Granada's hand might lead to a position of excessive market dominance and undue influence over ITV's 'Network Centre' which is responsible for commissioning and scheduling ITV's programmes. However, the Commission took the view that 'the protections built into the structure of the Network Centre to preserve its independence' were sufficient to allay any fears of potential abuses of market power resulting from the proposed mergers (2000: 20–1). In effect, Granada was spared an adverse public interest finding in respect of its position as dominant programme supplier within ITV.

As far as advertising was concerned, the Commission noted that the main concern expressed to it was that 'any of the mergers would materially enhance the market power of the merged entities in relation to their advertising customers' (2000: 3). Although ITV's share of total UK television advertising had fallen to just over 60 per cent in 1999, ITV is nonetheless the only commercial television channel in the UK that meets 'the needs of advertisers who seek mass audiences for national campaigns' (2000: 21). So, according to the Commission, advertising within ITV should be identified in economic terms as a distinct market segment. This implies an ongoing requirement to sustain competition in airtime sales within ITV, despite the growth of other competitors across the television industry.

At the time of the CC Report, competition within ITV was already pretty limited, in that each of the three main players – Carlton, Granada and UN&M – accounted for a share of around one-third of ITV's total net advertising revenue through their respective airtime sales subsidiaries. But the Commission concluded that there would be grounds for concern only if further consolidation 'were to result in one dominant [I]TV company significantly larger than the next' (2000: 3). The Commission favoured an outcome in which the two largest ITV companies would be broadly equal in stature and it was against allowing any merger that could result in a position of dominance in airtime sales for any one player. Such a position would be established, according to the Commission, 'if one company had both a share of ITV NAR significantly higher than the next largest *and controlled more than two of the four leading ITV licences*' (ibid.; my emphasis).

The notion that ITV's federal structure involved 'four leading licences' was a new one. It had been set out in Granada's submission to the Commission. But, as can be seen from Table 8.1, the advertising revenue of Granada's North-West of England licence, at 6.0 per cent, is really not far short of the 6.9 per cent accounted for by the South-East licence and, indeed, many commentators have tended to refer to 'five' majors within ITV in the past. Nonetheless, the Commission was persuaded that only four leading licences existed in ITV: one for the Midlands, one for the South-East of England and the two London licences. Granada's argument, accepted by the Commission, was that if the Carlton/UN&M merger went ahead, then three out of the four 'leading' ITV licences would belong to the same company, thus creating a position of excessive dominance.

By contrast, Granada's own proposals to acquire either Carlton or United News & Media were unlikely, in the Commission's view, to pose any threat to the public interest. If Granada went ahead with a bid for

TABLE 8.1   Breakdown of ITV advertising and UK television audience shares, 1999

| | Share of NAR (%) | Audience share (%) | Owner |
|---|---|---|---|
| Midlands | 10.0 | 4.7 | Carlton |
| London Weekday | 9.5 | 2.8 | Carlton |
| London Weekend | 7.2 | 2.0 | Granada |
| South-East England | 6.9 | 2.4 | UN&M |
| North-West England | 6.0 | 3.9 | Granada |
| East of England | 4.3 | 1.8 | UN&M |
| Yorkshire | 4.3 | 3.2 | Granada |
| Wales & the West | 3.5 | 2.3 | UN&M |
| Central Scotland | 2.8 | 1.9 | SMG |
| North-East England | 2.2 | 1.5 | Granada |
| South-West England | 1.3 | 0.8 | Carlton |
| Northern Ireland | 1.2 | 1.0 | Ulster TV |
| North of Scotland | 0.9 | 0.6 | SMG |
| Borders | 0.4 | 0.5 | Border TV |
| Total | 60.5 | 29.5 | |

Source: Granada, reproduced in the Competition Commission Report (2000: 76)

either of its main rivals then obligatory divestments would follow. For example, if Granada acquired Carlton, then it would be obliged to sell one or other of the London licences to comply with the 15 per cent upper audience limit and the stipulation that no single company may own both such licences in the 1996 Broadcasting Act. Alternatively, if Granada acquired United News & Media, then divestment of the Wales & the West licence would be necessary to comply with the 15 per cent upper audience limit. Either way, the one other remaining major ITV player would be free to acquire whichever licences Granada chose to divest itself of and the net outcome would be two large ITV companies broadly equal in stature.

According to the Commission, the Carlton/UN&M merger threatened the public interest because it would result in one potentially dominant player which was much larger than the second-biggest ITV company, Granada. So, the merger should only be permitted on condition that the enlarged company would divest of one 'leading' licence – that for the South-East of England (2000: 5). This ruling dealt a severe blow to Carlton since, of all United News & Media's television assets, the South-East of England ITV licence was obviously the most valuable and attractive (see Table 8.1).

The Minister for Trade and Industry, Stephen Byers, fully accepted the Commission's recommendations. So the upper limit of 25 per cent of NAR would no longer count but, in its place, a new stipulation would prevent any single company from owning more than two of ITV's four 'leading' licences. The announcement of the Commission's findings and Byers' verdict on them was followed swiftly by a flurry of negotiations as Carlton, United News & Media and Granada sorted out a settlement. Granada, with the upper hand, managed to acquire all of United News & Media's television assets except the Wales and the West ITV licence which Carlton subsequently acquired. This latest round of consolidation left Granada with a total audience share of some 14.8 per cent (and an advertising share of around 26.6 per cent) as compared with Carlton's audience share of around 10.6 per cent (and 24.3 per cent share of advertising revenues).

The Commission's finding that further consolidation of ITV ownership was acceptable was, of course, based purely and solely on competition grounds. Competition authorities have no remit to consider issues surrounding the need for media pluralism, regional diversity, etc. The ITC, on the other hand, as regulator for the commercial broadcasting sector, *is* charged with safeguarding pluralism through ensuring compliance with ownership rules set out in legislation and, where necessary, by carrying out a public interest assessment of mergers involving commercial broadcasters.

For its part, the ITC noted in its published views to the CC that, in the form proposed, none of the mergers would fit with the terms of existing legislation and policy. It expressed the view that, already, 'greater concentration amongst C3 [ITV] licensees has adversely affected the regional identity of the ITV services' and that the proposed mergers 'would make the ITC's task of ensuring regional diversity in ITV programming more difficult' (ITC, 2000). Even so, against a background of rapid developments in the broadcasting industry and pressure for structural change, the ITC pronounced that it was in favour of a general review of existing ownership legislation and '[i]n the meantime . . . was not opposed to some further concentration of C3 [ITV] ownership' (CC, 2000: 169).

The wider implication of the CC Report, endorsed by the ITC and accepted by the Minister for Trade and Industry, is that the Government now agreed that the time had come to allow further consolidation of ownership within the UK television industry. The CC's solution of allowing ITV to be controlled by two broadly equal large players appears to be only a stepping stone on the way to single ownership of the network – a destination which many regard as unavoidable so as to allow ITV streamline its strategic decision making (2000: 14). But, before ITV can be controlled by just one player, primary legislation is needed to sweep away the rules in the 1990 and 1996 Broadcasting Acts that limit any company's audience share to a maximum of 15 per cent and that prevent single ownership of both London ITV licences.

## White Paper on communications

A blueprint for new legislation emerged in December 2000 with the publication of a White Paper called *A New Future for Communications*. The White Paper represented the work of two Government Ministries – the Department of Culture Media, Media and Sport and the Department of Trade and Industry (DTI) – and it followed on from an earlier Green Paper entitled *Regulating Communications: Approaching Convergence in the Information Age* (1998). The main goal for new legislation, as implied in the title of the Green Paper, is to rationalize and co-ordinate regulation in the UK right across the 'converging' telecommunications and broadcasting sectors.

The key proposal in the White Paper is the creation of a single regulatory entity called OFCOM which will deal with content and economic issues for telecoms and broadcasting. OFCOM will replace the existing plethora of regulators (including the ITC, the Broadcasting Standards Commission, the Radio Authority, OFTEL, etc.) and introduce a more coherent and co-ordinated approach to regulation of communications across different sorts of delivery platforms in future. This restructuring of regulation is, indeed, radical and makes the UK one of the first countries to institute unified regulation across communications infrastructures and broadcasting.

The new regulatory approach favoured by the Government can be summarized as 'competition plus' – i.e. normal competition law provides the basic bedrock but various additional measures will be built onto this to tackle aspects of the media business that are 'special' (Harding, 2000b: 2–3; O'Connor, 2000: 3). The 1998 Competition Act and the monopoly provisions in the 1973 Fair Trading Act are key elements in the new framework for media regulation (DTI/DCMS: 2000: 13). On top of this, OFCOM will take responsibility for content regulation and spectrum management. In terms of broadcasting content, the Government proposes a new 'three-tier' approach with a basic tier of regulation concerning standards of taste and decency to govern all broadcasters and with additional, more demanding levels of content regulation that apply only to public service broadcasters.

The importance of competition is stressed throughout the White Paper. Under the new proposals, the competition authorities (the CC and OFT) will retain responsibility for communications and media as before but they will be expected to consult with OFCOM on mergers involving telecommunications or media players. OFCOM will itself be expected to promote competition and, as an additional safeguard for consumers, is to be given sector-specific powers to prevent any anticipated abuses of market power. The White Paper identifies the potential for vertical concentrations of ownership in communications markets as a particular threat, but it shies away from banning or restricting vertical integration between content providers and owners of distribution networks (2000: 16). Instead, OFCOM will be given special powers to ensure that, where market dominance occurs, open access for rival content providers and rival networks will be maintained.

A strengthened approach towards regulation of competition within and across the various sectors of the UK communications and media industries will be welcomed by many. In the UK media sector, many allegations or instances of abuse of market power have had to be investigated by the competition authorities in recent years (e.g. aggressive pricing strategies in the newspaper industry, or monopolized control over distribution of feature films, or 'gateway' monopolies in broadcasting, or bundling of pay-television channels, or conditional selling in advertising markets). However, few such inquiries have resulted in decisive interventions to bring about restructuring or to eliminate anti-competitive behaviour. In the telecommunications sector, OFTEL's performance in sustaining open competition – especially in relation to BT's reticence about unbundling the local loop[2] – has also been criticized as less than effective.

More effective measures to sustain open competition will undoubtedly help encourage diversity and pluralism. As the White Paper rightly proclaims, '[f]ostering competition is the first step to promoting plurality in the media' (2000: 36). But, of course, competition and pluralism are not the same thing. The White Paper acknowledges that competitive markets will not necessarily guarantee diversity of content and a diversity of owners or 'voices'. So, the Government suggests that '[g]iven the democratic importance of the media . . . we may continue to need backstop powers to underpin plurality of ownership and a plurality of views in the media' (ibid.).

What exactly those 'backstop powers' will be is a vital question which remains unanswered. The White Paper provides some clues. An entire chapter is devoted to 'Maintaining diversity and pluralism'. The main suggestions under this heading, aside from plans to relax ownership rules, involve retaining the compulsory 25 per cent access quota for independent producers, retaining regional programming obligations imposed on public service broadcasters and reviewing possibilities to extend local community broadcasting. The continuation of the Government's commitment both to independent programme production and to regional and local programme services should, indeed, help to promote diversity of content. But what about 'plurality of ownership'?

On the specific issue of ownership, the main proposals are, first, to replace the 15 per cent upper audience limit for television broadcasters and revoke the rule banning single ownership of the two London ITV licences and, second, to simplify or do away with the current points system that limits ownership of radio broadcasting to a 15 per cent share of commercial audiences (2000: 35). These suggested changes will allow unprecedented opportunities for major commercial radio and television broadcasters to expand and consolidate their share of the UK market. Clearly, then, the promised 'reforms' are more likely to increase rather than to reduce concentrations of ownership in the UK radio and television broadcasting sectors.

The reason why the 15 per cent upper limit on market share in the television industry needs to go is, according to the White Paper, because many responses to the Green Paper, 'including that from the ITC, argued that the rule is more restrictive than is now necessary ... given the increasing range of services now available'. This viewpoint ignores the fact that the number of television services now licensed by the ITC far exceeds the range of services actually watched by most UK viewers. Nevertheless, according to the White Paper, the time has come to lift all restrictions on ownership of commercial television except, perhaps, the ban on joint ownership of ITV plus Channel 5 (2000: 41). Likewise, plans to simplify or abolish the points system that limits ownership of radio broadcasting reflect the Government's sympathy with arguments put forward by the radio industry that companies ought to be given 'greater scope for investment and achieving economies of scale' (ibid.).

As far as pluralism is concerned, there are, of course, some grounds for concern, particularly in relation to the implied loss of regional diversity and autonomy as ownership of ITV and of local radio consolidates even further. On the other hand, some would argue that proposals to retain a strong commitment through OFCOM to the regional dimension of licensed television and radio services are sufficient to counteract the effects of more concentrated ownership. Many seem convinced that further consolidation of ITV ownership will make no difference. One rival television broadcaster is blunt in his dismissal of the benefits of ITV's federal structure:

> Why have several [ITV] companies all redistributing *Coronation Street* with several sets of costs? Because that is all that they do. They are only there because it was the Government's half-baked attempt to prevent monopolies, but monopolies are there anyway because they screw the advertisers and abuse their power ... [I]n whatever ITV region you're in you still have to watch the same channel, so it is half-baked ...

As discussed in Part II, further monomedia expansion by UK commercial television and radio broadcasters should allow for a range of economic benefits. For example, allowing further consolidation of ITV ownership can clearly be justified on efficiency grounds to the extent that the network's programme service can be delivered more cost-effectively by one rather than several regional owners. However, the implications in terms of competition in advertising markets need to be considered and, as far wider economic welfare is concerned, a key test is what impact consolidation of radio or television ownership is likely to have on the total value gained by listeners and viewers from broadcast services. In order to favour the public interest, consolidation of ownership must be achieved without any reduction in aggregate listener or viewer welfare.

A few, but not many, responses to the new proposals in the White Paper have highlighted worries about the potential for loss of pluralism and regional diversity. The Essex Campaign for Local Radio, for example, argued that consolidation of ownership encourages networking and greater uniformity of output at the expense of local diversity. The Campaign for Press and Broadcasting Freedom pointed out that the new proposals 'promote further concentration of ownership in communications' and argued that, to preserve pluralism and democracy, '[t]his position should be reversed' by retaining and strengthening existing rules on monomedia and cross-media ownership (CPBF, 2001: 4).

However, the view that further consolidation of ownership within UK commercial broadcasting is to be welcomed was much more strongly represented amongst responses to the White Paper. The majority of views submitted on the question of deregulating ownership provisions came, not surprisingly, from large broadcasters. Deregulation of radio ownership was supported by players such as GWR, EMAP and Scottish Radio Holdings, not least on the grounds that this would bring constraints on ownership in this sector into line with limitations on ownership of television. Deregulation of television ownership was favoured by leading commercial players such as Granada. Even the BBC, in its response to the White Paper, asserts that 'the UK's interests are best served by a regime which encourages the development of commercial media players able to operate globally, boost exports and support strong growth in the creative economy at home'. The corporation therefore 'welcomes the Government's conclusion that further consolidation might be allowed within the broadcast marketplace – including ownership of ITV and local radio stations' (BBC, 2001: 6).

In addition to sweeping away monomedia ownership ceilings for broadcasters, the White Paper proposes introducing a 'lighter touch' approach to newspaper mergers and it asked for views on whether cross-media ownership restrictions ought to be 'reformed' (DTI/DCMS, 2000: 35, 41). In particular, comments were invited on whether rules that prevent newspaper owners with a national market share of more than 20 per cent from also having a controlling interest in terrestrial television and radio broadcasting licences should now be relaxed. The White Paper acknowledges that '[m]any have called for the current cross-media ownership rules to be revoked' but, at the same time, it points out that '[c]ross-media consolidations which are desirable on economic grounds may tend to reduce the plurality of viewpoints and sources of information available' (2000: 42).

One possibility, according to the Government, might be to resurrect the notion of a regulatory model based on 'share of voice' (2000: 42–3). The idea of replacing cross-media ownership rules with an approach based on a common upper limit of the 'total' media market for players in all sectors was originally proposed by the Conservative Government in the 1995 Green Paper on media ownership (DNH, 1995a). The 1995 proposals suggested moving to a system in which the total media market would be defined, an upper limit for ownership would be set and a means found for calculating and reflecting the varying levels of influence represented by different media sectors (an 'exchange rate') so that all media owners would be constrained to a common upper limit or share of voice. Implementation of these commendable but ambitious proposals was beset by many practical difficulties and, in the end, the 'share of voice' idea was abandoned ahead of the 1996 legislation as too contentious.

Undaunted by the setbacks experienced in 1995, New Labour's vision of *A New Future for Communications* raises the possibility that a share of voice approach might now be better suited to market conditions than existing cross-media rules (DTI/DCMS, 2000: 42–3). Indeed, the sub-section devoted to cross-ownership is one of the parts of the White Paper that attracted most responses (Graham, 2001: 5). But, once again, views appear to be divided on the merits of a share of voice measure. Amongst those who showed some interest in switching to such an approach, there was little consensus about how shares should be aggregated across different media sectors. How, for example, should $x$ per cent share of the television audience compare with $y$ per cent of newspaper circulations? Should $x$ per cent of the television audience be given a heavier weighting than $x$ per cent of the radio audience? And how should new media, especially the Internet, be included in the calculation of a media owner's share of voice?

Some would suggest that, '[s]ince 1996, the philosophical case for this [share of voice] approach has become more compelling, as online media and multi-channel television have spread' (I. Hargreaves, 2000: 5). Hargreaves believes that practical difficulties in implementing the media share approach are 'not insuperable'. He has proposed setting an overall limit on share of media voice at 10 per cent (which coincides with what was suggested in the 1995 Green Paper on media ownership) and believes that the best way to calculate and weigh up the relative shares for different media such as newspapers, radio channels and websites is by measuring time spent consuming each medium.

Associated Newspapers, in its submission responding to the White Paper proposals, was also of the view that upper restraints on cross-ownership ought to be judged by reference to share of voice '[c]alculated on a basis giving equal weight to each form of media consumption' (Associated Newspapers, 2001: 9). Beyond this, however, Associated Newspapers offered little advice on what the upper limit for share of voice ought to be or precisely which media ought to be included.

Others are sceptical about the share of voice approach. Barnett suggests that attempts to measure diversity by using such an approach are 'a methodological nonsense' (Barnett, 2001: 3). He argues that systems for aggregating shares of newspaper reading, television viewing and radio listening – usually promoted by media companies that want to diversify – fail to take into account obligations for broadcasters (but not newspapers) to remain neutral and they tend to rely on unproven assumptions about the relative influence of different media. This point about different cultures of impartiality between the press and broadcasting is echoed elsewhere. Granada's submission highlights the fact that broadcast media are subject to extensive regulation to ensure the impartiality of news services whereas, by contrast, there is a strong tradition of political partisanship in the newspaper sector. Consequently, according to Granada, consolidation of newspapers and broadcast media still needs to be restricted in the interest of protecting plurality (Granada, 2001: 15).

Several responses to the cross-ownership proposals were, predictably enough, from large newspaper publishers and trade associations such as the Newspaper Society. Few warmed to the notion of a new share of voice approach. Instead, most argued simply that '[c]ross media ownership controls must be liberalised' (Newspaper Society, 2001: 2). Scottish Media Group expressed the belief that 'to continue to restrict cross media ownership is counter-productive as it undermines the stability of all but the largest media owners' (SMG, 2001: 7). Trinity Mirror suggested that the 20 per cent upper limit is outdated and that 'any percentage restriction on cross-media ownership . . . would be entirely subjective in detail' (2001: 2). According to News International, '[t]he variety of ways in which consumers receive news, [etc.] . . . is increasing almost daily. And no group dominates, or can hope to dominate all the pathways to the public' (NI, 2001: 4). So, according to these industry players, cross-media ownership restrictions can safely be removed.

In contrast with the boldness of the Government's proposals in the White Paper to liberalise television and radio monomedia ownership restrictions, relatively little has been said about exactly which direction will be taken on the politically sensitive question of cross-media ownership. Several references are made to the greater choice and diversity of services made possible by new communication technologies. The suggestion is made that '[p]lurality concerns may diminish as more people gain access to the range of services now available on digital TV and radio and the Internet' (DTI/DCMS, 2000: 42). But the White Paper also acknowledges that, despite the growth in electronic communications, most people still rely on a handful of mainstream television channels and national newspapers for the majority of their information, political analysis and entertainment. With astute political timing, the Government's decision to invite further consultation on cross-ownership deferred the need to adopt a position on this thorny issue until well after the general election in June 2001.

### Back to the future

The Government's plans to rationalize media regulation and 'to safeguard the interests of citizens and consumers', while at the same time making the UK 'home to the most dynamic and competitive communications market in the world' over coming years (DTI/DCMS, 2000: 3) are commendably ambitious. The move to introduce a single coherent approach to regulation across telecommunications and broadcasting will address many areas of inconsistency and regulatory overlap. Provided that proper account is taken of sectoral differences within the communications industry, OFCOM's arrival will be a welcome step. The Government's renewed commitment to public service broadcasting, universal access, quality and diversity is broadly encouraging and its plans to move to more flexible regulation of commercial players offer a sensible response to recent market developments. In addition, proposals for more effective sector-specific regulation of competition in telecommunications and broad-casting markets should help encourage wider market access and greater diversity.

But there still remains the problem of ensuring a plurality of different voices in the UK media. Despite a cornucopia of new digital services and growth of the Internet, concentrated ownership of the main instruments of mass communication is undeniably a dangerous and undesirable state of affairs. Current media consumption patterns confirm that most UK adults still derive the majority of their news and views from just a few predominant channels. The principal risk associated with allowing these predominant avenues of mass communication to fall into the hands of only a few players is that some political views or forms of cultural expression (those favoured by influential owners) will be over-represented while others are sidelined or left out of the mainstream media.

The obvious example of where failure to curb excesses of media power can lead to is provided by Italian media magnate Silvio Berlusconi who, in May 2001, managed to get elected as Prime Minister of Italy for the second time. In the period preceding the election, Mr Berlusconi used his extensive media interests to blatantly promote his own political campaign, and his *Rete Quattro* television channel, whose evening news had become 'tantamount to a Berlusconi propaganda rally', was censured by the Communications Authority for breaching rules on political impartiality (Betts, 2001: 6). Alignments of corporate media and political power may not often be as boldly explicit as this but they nonetheless flourish when major concentrations of media ownership are allowed to occur. In the UK, a major newspaper proprietor who takes the view that, for example, the UK should not join the Euro, is well placed to generate a climate of public opinion that is hostile to such a move. This state of affairs is damaging to democracy and profoundly undermines the wider public interest.

Since a reliance on competition law has so obviously failed to prevent the accumulation of excessive concentrations of media power in the UK newspaper industry, it is difficult to feel confident that switching from upper ownership limits to a competition-based approach in broadcasting markets – as is suggested in the White Paper – will achieve any better results in the television or radio sectors. A regulatory approach to ownership based primarily on competition and on economic and commercial considerations is not designed, first and foremost, to protect pluralism and democracy. But pluralism needs to be protected by restrictions on media ownership because, as many commentators have pointed out, '[w]hen misallocations of market power occur in media, the result is the corrosion of our civic life' (I. Hargreaves, 2001: 5).

In many respects, the issue of curbing media power seems once again to have been ducked. Rather than introducing measures to tackle the predominance of News International in the daily newspaper sector, it seems that the rules are once again being adjusted to try to encourage domestic players to rival the expansionist strategies that have earned News International its success. And the White Paper makes no mention whatsoever of any dangers or disadvantages that may be posed by allowing commercial television and radio broadcasters to dramatically extend their shares of ownership or 'voice' in respective markets in the near future.

The important remaining test is what will be done about cross-ownership. The regulatory measures that prevent major newspaper publishers from also having a controlling interest in terrestrial broadcasting licences now appear to represent one of the very few protections for plurality of media ownership that could survive into the 'New Future for Communications'. In theory, cross-ownership restrictions could be made more effective if, as mooted in the White Paper, the basis for these were switched to an overall share of voice measurement. Whatever about altering the basis for calculating cross-ownership, the more far-reaching question is whether the Government is prepared to stand firm against industrial pressures to do away with such restrictions altogether.

The economic efficiency and performance of media industry players may be strongly influenced by ownership constraints. Certainly, it is desirable that media ownership policy should encourage the economic strength of domestic media and communications sectors. But whether combined ownership of newspaper publishing plus broadcasting interests confers any significant positive economic benefits is highly questionable. In any event, economic considerations are by no means the only or the most important public interest concerns tied up with cross-media ownership policy. If the Government carries on facilitating the interests and ambitions of major UK commercial media players at the expense of safeguards for pluralism, what is at stake is the ability to prevent powerful corporate media interests, UK-based or otherwise from predominating over political decision-making in future.

---

## Notes

1. The full text of Chris Smith's speech to the RTS is posted on the DCMS website at http://www.gov.uk

2. The process of 'unbundling the local loop' refers to providing access for competing providers of high-bandwith services to BT's local telephone exchanges and lines.

# IV

# Media Ownership Policy in Europe

# 9

# Trends and Policy Responses across Europe

Tendencies towards expansion and diversification in the media are an international phenomenon. As we saw earlier, concentration trends are fuelled by a wide range of economic and commercial motives that apply to media proprietors everywhere. Consequently, many examples of mergers, acquisitions and other strategic alliances involving large media and communications firms can be found in virtually every country in Europe. Issues surrounding convergence and concentrations of media ownership have, in turn, worked their way onto the national policy agenda in most European countries over recent years and have also captured the attention of European Union policy-makers.

Recent evidence of national and transnational corporate expansion within Europe by European and US media suppliers is plentiful. But there is uncertainty about whether concentrated media ownership is a national or a European policy question. Confusion arises because, notwithstanding progress towards a single European market, the structure of media provision in Europe still reflects a predominantly national focus. The 'European' media market is comprised not of a unified or cross-integrated system of provision for a collective audience but of a somewhat notional or artificial aggregation of the markets of each individual member state. And problems arise with embarking on a harmonized approach to media ownership, not least because each member state – irrespective of how small a proportion it represents of the collective 'European' market – is conscious of domestic pluralism within what its continues to regard as its own market, i.e. its national territory. Moreover, each country in Europe is concerned with setting a framework at the national level which promotes the position of its own indigenous media and communications players in what is seen as an increasingly competitive and global media marketplace.

This chapter and the next are devoted to examining the media owner-ship policy situation in Europe. The current chapter traces recent trends in ownership within and across a range of European countries. It considers how concentrations of ownership have affected pluralism in Europe and, drawing on examples, it explains the different sorts of approach taken towards regulating media ownership and promoting pluralism. Chapter 10 then focuses on policy developments at the collective pan-European level and, in particular, it analyses the European Union's efforts to introduce an integrated transnational approach towards regulating media concentrations.

## Media ownership trends in Europe

The Council of Europe, which is responsible for ensuring compliance with the European Convention on Human Rights, has long taken an interest in how media concentrations across Europe may affect pluralism and, in turn, freedom of speech. To assist its work in this area, the Council established a Committee of Experts on Media Concentrations and Pluralism (MM-CM), and throughout the 1990s this Committee gathered information about patterns of media ownership in Europe and about the implications for pluralism. Reports compiled by a network of national correspondents on behalf of MM-CM provide a useful account of media ownership trends in the different countries of Europe (Council of Europe, 1997b). These reports suggest that whereas some Eastern European countries such as Latvia and the Slovak Republic have been characterized by a trend towards increased diversity of media supply (as new owners and new products enter the marketplace), the prevalent tendency across the majority of European countries appears to be one of high and increasing levels of media and cross-media concentration.

In Germany, for example, revisions of the Broadcasting State Treaty were followed, throughout the late 1990s, by higher levels of concentrated ownership in the television sector. A small number of dominant players (especially Bertelsmann, Kirch, Bauer, Holtzbrinck and WAZ-Gruppe) control extensive cross-media empires and the tendency towards cross-sectoral media domination appears to be on the increase, with existing large owners also predominating in the development of new digital television services (Kleinwächter, 1998: 35–44). An attempted merger in the pay-TV sector involving Kirch, Bertelsmann and Deutsche Telekom in 1998 was vetoed only after intervention by the EC because of concerns about excessive market dominance. Undeterred, Kirch and others have continued in their efforts to expand (Benoit, 2001: 30).

Likewise in the UK, ownership of regional ITV television services has continued to consolidate rapidly in recent years. Whereas some might have hoped that the introduction of digital broadcasting from 1998 onwards would have increased diversity of ownership, this has not really been the case. The consortium awarded control over new digital terrestrial television channels was comprised of the two largest existing ITV companies – Carlton Television and Granada Group – and this enterprise sources much of its 'premium' digital content from the largest existing satellite broadcaster in the UK – BSkyB. So, expansion in the range of channels available in the UK in recent years has not been matched by increased diversity of ownership.

Meanwhile, levels of ownership in the UK national and regional press and in the commercial radio sector (as measured by the share of audience or readership held by the largest owners) have become more concentrated in recent years. And levels of cross-sectoral media domination have increased thanks to mergers between, for example, broadcasters and newspaper publishers (e.g. SMG's acquisition of Caledonian Newspapers and Grampian Television in the late 1990s and its investments in the commercial radio sector since 2000) or between newspaper and magazine publishers (e.g. magazine publisher Northern & Shell's acquisition of Express Newspapers from UN&M in November 2000).

At the same time, several UK media firms have been expanding operations internationally. Media conglomerate EMAP, for example, acquired several magazine publishing operations in France in the mid-1990s and has since expanded heavily into the US market. Pearson, which merged its television operations with CLT-Ufa in 2000 to form pan-European television company RTL subsequently went on to forge alliances in Hong Kong to facilitate its expansion in Asia (Harding, 2000a: 25). Many players from other European countries have also successfully pursued strategies of transnational expansion. For example, the French media, communications and utility group Vivendi merged with Canadian film and music company Seagram (owner of Universal) in autumn 2000 to create a transatlantic media empire valued at some $34 billion (D. Hargreaves, 2000a: 21).

Levels of cross-ownership between newspaper publishing and broadcasting have increased in several other European countries in recent years. In Portugal, for example, the SOCI publishing group acquired a national radio station as well as a stake in television broadcaster TV1 in 1996–97. In Sweden, the Bonnier group, which already accounts for a 25 per cent share of Swedish press circulations, acquired a significant stake in Sweden's second-largest television broadcaster, TV4 in the late 1990s. The Bonnier group extended its media operations horizontally into the UK in autumn

2000 with the launch of a new daily newspaper called *Business AM* in Scotland.

Meanwhile in Norway, leading national and regional newspaper publisher A-pressen has recently been extending its television activities. The Norwegian press sector provides another good example of trans-national European media expansion. Orkla, which is the third-largest Norwegian press company and has interests in the domestic television and advertising sectors, expanded overseas into the Polish daily newspaper market by buying up stakes in several regional newspapers and magazines as well as by taking a 51 per cent shareholding in national title *Rzeczpospolita* in the late 1990s. Orkla is now one of the largest press companies in Poland. Diversity of ownership of the Polish press sector also diminished in the 1996–97 period as another foreign publisher, German company Passau Neue Presse, raised the number of Polish regional daily titles it controls from 8 to 11. Strong competition from increasingly concentrated press groups in Poland has, in some cases, resulted in the demise of existing newspaper titles. In the summer of 1997, for example, four newspapers were liquidated including two national dailies, *Sztander* and *Slovo*.

Likewise, the closure of two daily newspapers in Cyprus – *Elefthero-typia* and *Vima Tis Kyprou* – reflected generally increased levels of concentration of ownership in the press sector in the late 1990s. The demise of these two 'centre ground' newspapers left only right-wing and left-wing papers amongst the remaining eight titles in the market. Cyprus has no regional press. In effect, middle-ground views were no longer represented or available in any daily newspapers in Cyprus following these closures.

In Switzerland, which is divided into three distinct linguistic regions, greater concentration of press ownership has led to the disappearance of some regional titles and it has become increasingly common to find *de facto* monopolies in every canton or economic area. In order to improve their profitability, regional newspapers have been pooling their strengths either through mergers or close collaboration agreements.

In Iceland, diversity in the press sector was reduced considerably in the late 1990s by the merger of two daily titles (*Dagur* and *Timinn*) and the closure of another. By 1997, the number of daily newspapers in Iceland was down to only three and there is extensive cross-ownership between the press and broadcasting sectors. Because the three dominant commercial media suppliers are interconnected through cross-ownership, there have effectively been only two separate and autonomous 'voices' in the Icelandic media – the Islenka utvarpsfelagid/ Frjals fjolnidlun/ Arvakur amalga-mation and the state-run Icelandic Broadcasting Company.

In short, trends from the latter half of the 1990s onwards suggest that, even though new avenues for distribution of media are developing rapidly, the number of separate and autonomous companies responsible for supplying what are currently the most widely consumed media is, in very many European countries, standing still or *contracting* rather than increasing. A counter-trend was reported by MM-CM's network of correspondents in some of the markets of Eastern Europe (e.g. Latvia) where, following the demise of monopolistic state control over the media in the early 1990s, ownership was still becoming more diverse in the late 1990s. However, in both large and small European countries, many examples can be found of dominant media enterprises actually strengthening their market positions in recent years.

Part of the explanation for existing patterns of media ownership and output in Europe may reside in the fact that larger markets or wealthier member states can generally afford a more diverse provision of media than smaller ones. As discussed in Chapter 2, the larger and wealthier member states of Europe such as France, Germany and Italy can and often do support a greater overall number of suppliers and a greater diversity of media output than smaller or poorer member states such as Greece or Portugal. But several counter-examples exist of high levels of diversity in small Northern European markets and, indeed, large and powerful media conglomerates thrive in virtually all of Europe's wealthiest markets, such as News International in the UK, Bertelsmann in Germany or Fininvest in Italy. Even so, the EU member states with the greatest concentrations of press ownership at present are both very small – Luxembourg and Ireland.

The predominant player in Ireland's media sector is Tony O' Reilly, Chairman of Independent News & Media and owner of a 27 per cent stake in Independent Newspapers. Independent Newspapers accounts for a market share of in excess of 70 per cent of print media in Ireland through national titles including the *Irish Independent, Sunday Independent, Sunday World* and *Evening Herald* as well as a range of regional titles (Dinan, 2001: 9). O'Reilly also has a 50 per cent interest in Princes Holdings, owner of Ireland's second-largest cable television operator, Irish Multichannel. Independent Newspapers' empire is not confined to Ireland but includes 'newspaper and magazine publishing, digital media and outdoor advertising in the UK, France, South Africa, Australia and New Zealand' (2001: 9).

Another factor which accounts for unequal levels of media concentration across Europe is the disparity in public policy that exists from one territory to another. Whereas many countries (e.g. the UK, Germany, France and Italy) favour restrictions on the market share or number of broadcast licences held by individual media owners, some (e.g. Norway) prefer to adopt a public interest test approach to particular instances of concentrated media ownership, and others rely on content regulation (e.g. Poland) or on self-regulatory measures to promote editorial independence from media owners (e.g. Switzerland). Some countries (e.g. Austria, Belgium, Finland, Norway and Sweden) provide direct subsidies to promote diversity in the print media whereas others do not, and some (e.g. the UK) provide subsidies for broadcast services targeted at specific minority groups. So, for example, the fact that levels of concentration of ownership of national daily newspapers in the UK are exceptionally high for such a large market and are relatively low in the smaller national markets of Norway and Sweden is largely a reflection of disparities in public policy towards the press in these different countries.

The convergence of telecommunications, broadcasting and Internet technologies has undoubtedly played a major role in encouraging some of the mergers and alliances that have taken place across Europe in recent years. According to Hughes, convergence has led us into 'a new era of consolidation and mega-mergers such as AOL's effective takeover of Time Warner', with the US well in the lead and Europe struggling to keep up (2000: 7). Many recent domestic and transnational deals in Europe straddle both traditional and 'new' media and involve both content creation and distribution. For example, the $5.5 billion acquisition of one of Europe's largest television programme producers, Danish company Endemol, by Spanish telecommunications operator Telefónica in 2000 was clearly intended to create a major vertically integrated media and communications entity. Telecom Italia attempted a similar strategy when its ISP subsidiary Seat Pagine Gialle tried to acquire broadcaster Telemontecarlo in 2000 but was prevented under Italian legislation on cross-ownership (Kapner, 2001: 29). In April 2001, a consortium led by Ireland's largest media owner, Tony O' Reilly, made a bid for the country's former state-owned telecommunications operator, Eircom in a deal expected to create substantial synergies between content production and distribution capabilities (Roberts and Brown, 2001: 1).

## Implications for pluralism

The increasing prevalence of marriages of this sort between media content creation and communications infrastructure provision raises inevitable concerns about market dominance and about pluralism. As Hughes notes, '[w]hile technological innovation is increasing the number of delivery channels, vertical consolidation is reducing the number of channels to the market' (2000: 37). High and increasing levels of media concentration within and across European national markets can readily be accounted for in terms of economic, commercial and other strategic benefits but they also pose serious concerns about how to maintain open, diverse and pluralistic systems of media provision.

The main problem as regards pluralism is, as discussed earlier, a heightened risk of over-representation of certain political viewpoints or values or certain forms of cultural output at the expense of others. Some argue that what counts is whether dominant owners actually do interfere in editorial decisions or 'whether editorial autonomy is guaranteed' (De Bens and Ostbye, 1998: 13). It may be that in some instances of consolidated ownership, editorial functions and consumer choices will not be affected and, therefore, it may be argued that pluralism is not damaged. However, the problem with concentrated ownership is the *risk* of direct or indirect influence over content and agenda, irrespective of whether, in practice, many or most media owners try to cause a predominance of certain forms of output.

Plentiful evidence exists across Europe that, in some cases at least, concentrations of ownership do result in interference and greater standardization of output. The Berlusconi case in Italy is, perhaps, the most notorious instance of a causal connection between concentrated media ownership and an undesirable narrowing in the diversity of political opinions available to the public via the media. But the relationship between concentrations and pluralism is complicated. Sometimes, large media groups find themselves in a better position to provide diversity of content (through strategies of market segmentation) than small firms. At other times, diversity of ownership does not result in a diversity of voices because rival owners choose to rely on exactly the same sources of content. So, whether European concentrations of ownership actually result in greater diversity or a greater uniformity of output often depends on individual circumstances.

A multiplicity of suppliers is obviously desirable in many ways, but it may not be enough to guarantee an open and diverse system of media provision. Clearly, pluralism also depends on diversity of media content. Concentrated control over the 'upstream' activity of content production can be as potentially threatening to media diversity as concentrated ownership of distribution activities – e.g. broadcasting or newspaper publishing. This raises special concerns about the emergence of a new generation of powerful vertically integrated communications players such as AOL/Time Warner who, as noted by Oliver, can use their control over 'key content' to ensure their continued dominance across any new distribution platforms that happen to emerge (2000: 64). The increasing complexity surrounding opportunities to monopolise the supply chain for media has presented a considerable challenge for national policy-makers across Europe.

## Policies on media ownership and pluralism in Europe

The general conviction that diversity or plurality of media is a legitimate goal for public policy seems to be widely exemplified across Europe insofar as a majority of countries have enshrined policy measures to safeguard or promote media pluralism in their own domestic legislation (CE, 1996). In common with the UK, most member states of the European Union impose some special restrictions on ownership of the media over and above safeguards provided by domestic or EU competition law. The existence of these special measures reflects a recognition of the unique role that a diverse and pluralistic system of media provision plays in sustaining cultural diversity, social cohesion and democracy.

It is difficult to summarize the nature of media ownership restrictions for the whole of the European Union because these have evolved separately under the jurisdiction of each member state and in accordance with the characteristics of each county's media markets. Not only do upper thresholds on media and cross-media ownership vary widely from one member state to the next, but even the broad approach towards regulation of media ownership tends to differ. While some countries such as the UK, France and Germany have opted for mechanistic upper limits on ownership, others such as Sweden favour a public interest test approach, allowing each instance of concentrated ownership to be considered and dealt with on a case-by-case basis.

Upper ceilings on ownership represent the most widely adopted approach, but the basis for measurement of ownership tends to vary. As discussed earlier, '[d]etermining a media company's political and cultural influence presents unusually difficult problems of measurement' (Shew and Stelzer, 1996: 126) and a number of differences in approach can be found across Europe. In Germany and the UK, the basis for calculation of media market share is audiences but the benchmark adopted elsewhere (such as in Italy) sometimes involves shares of media revenue.

In France, rules exist which limit monomedia ownership in the television, radio and press sectors. These restrictions were, to some extent, relaxed in the mid-1990s when upper restrictions on permitted levels of shareholdings in television services were increased from 25 per cent to 49 per cent. At the same time, maximum audience thresholds for ownership of commercial radio broadcasting licences were also substantially increased (CE, 1997a: 40–1). Even so, a 'complex set' of monomedia and cross-media restrictions still apply in France (DTI/DCMS, 2000: 43) and restrictions on 'foreign' ownership prevent non-nationals from owning more than 20 per cent of any French newspaper publisher (CE, 1996: 21).

Ownership of the press in France is limited by rules that prevent anyone from controlling titles that account for in excess of 30 per cent of the daily newspaper market (CE, 1996: 25). Likewise, in Italy, national legislation prevents any individual or company from controlling a market share of more than 20 per cent of the national press or 50 per cent in any given region. Such limits are, in theory, all well and good but they have not always succeeded in preventing powerful empires from developing in the press sector. In France, for example, the four most important publishers of national daily newspapers (Socpresse, Group Le Monde, SAIP and Group Les Echos) accounted for a combined market share of some 83 per cent in 1995.[1]

In Germany, the approach taken towards regulation of press ownership is similar to the UK in that no upper limits have been set down in statute law; instead, mergers and acquisitions involving print media publishers that exceed a certain level are notified to the competition authorities – in this case, the Federal Cartel Office – for investigation. Under Germany's Act against Restraints of Competition, the usual reference threshold that applies to mergers in general (of a combined annual turnover in excess of DM 500 million) is reduced in the case of newspaper and magazine mergers to a threshold of combined turnover in excess of DM 25 million per annum (CE, 1996: 40). However, the approach taken by the Federal Cartel Office has been criticized as excessively non-interventionist and, again, highly concentrated levels of ownership have been allowed to accumulate across the German newspaper industry (Humphreys, 1996: 96).

A new Broadcasting Treaty which came into force in Germany in 1997 relaxed previous restrictions on ownership of broadcasting companies and switched the basis of these from number of services owned to audience share. Individual companies may now control licences covering up to a 30 per cent share of the German television audience (CE, 1997a: 43). Cross-ownership restrictions also apply. Under the 'viewer share' model adopted, companies are prevented from controlling broadcasting or press interests that, in total, give the company a degree of influence equivalent to more than a 30 per cent share of the television audience in Germany. According to Kleinwächter, this regulatory structure allows 'three big players up to 30 per cent (in practice Kirch, Bertelsmann and public broadcasting) with a remainder of a little more than 10 per cent for different minority groups' (1998: 55).

In Ireland, no statutory limits on media ownership currently exist but the Radio and Television Act 1988 requires the regulatory authority for commercial broadcasting (the Independent Radio and Television Commission) to consider, when awarding radio broadcasting licences, the desirability of allowing undue levels of control over the media to occur (Dinan, 2001: 2). Ownership of the press is not subject to any special rules or regulations, but the distinct characteristics of the press and the need for plurality of ownership were specifically acknowledged in a report from the Competitions and Mergers Review Group (CMRG) to the Government in 2000. It is expected that this may result in authority over media mergers being vested in the Minister for Enterprise, Trade and Employment rather than in the general competition authorities in future (2001: 6).

Disparities in regulation of concentrations of media ownership at the national level across Europe tend to reflect wider differences in the approaches taken historically at the national level towards media and press regulation. Divergent regulation also reflects individual market circumstances and differences in the level of resources available to support diverse media ownership. One thing, however, which various domestic media ownership regimes within the EU seem to have in common is their exposure to persistent industrial calls for deregulation since the early 1990s. This pressure reflects a competitive impetus on the part of dominant indigenous players in the communications industries to participate in an ever-increasing international trend towards concentrations of media and cross-media ownership (MacLeod, 1996).

The deregulation of anti-concentration provisions in the United States through the Telecommunications Act 1996 has facilitated this international trend towards enlarged, transnational vertically and diagonally integrated media organizations and many European member states have followed suit. France introduced relaxations on concentrations on ownership in the television and the radio sectors in 1994. Italy also revised its approach to media ownership regulation in the mid-1990s. Likewise, Germany overhauled and deregulated domestic rules on cross-media media ownership in 1997. The UK instigated a substantial liberalization of rules on television ownership and on cross-ownership of press and broadcasting in the 1996 Broadcasting Act. Further deregulatory measures are to be introduced in the UK in the forthcoming Communications Act of 2002 or 2003 (DTI/DCMS, 2000: 35).

What exists in Europe at present, then, is a patchwork of media ownership regulations which have been determined at member state level in order to accommodate the circumstances and characteristics of domestic media provision in each country. This situation has led to concerns, some of which reflect the possibility that regulatory disparities obstruct cross-border investment in European media, and others of which surround the threat to pluralism posed by the development of national and transnational European media conglomerates such as News International, Bertelsmann, Hachette or Fininvest. Inevitably, such concerns have brought media ownership regulation onto the pan-European policy agenda. The collective response, under the auspices of the European Union, is discussed in some detail in the next chapter.

But ownership rules are by no means the only policy instrument used by Europe's national governments to tackle media concentrations and to promote pluralism. The development of new communication technologies has had a marked effect on the supply chain for media and on patterns of ownership and control of the media in recent years (Prosser et al., 1996). Conventional ownership rules based exclusively on 'traditional' media have, to some extent, been overtaken by developments surrounding digitization, convergence and the growth of the Internet, and national policy-makers have to respond accordingly.

A key concern surrounding advances in communications technologies is the potential for new patterns of cross-sectoral and/or vertical control to inhibit points of access to the media. Regulating 'gateways' and potential bottlenecks (e.g. monopoly control over conditional access systems, or user navigation systems or key content) has become pivotal to the objective of ensuring open and diverse systems of media provision. Imposing ownership restrictions too early on emerging media might deter investment and so prove counter-productive in terms of promoting diversity. On the other hand, the competition-based policy approach, with its emphasis on behavioural rather than structural interventions, has provided national regulators with an ideal alternative framework for dealing with gateways and bottlenecks. So, adopting this approach – where regulation aims to reduce the possibility of abuses of a dominant position rather than to eliminate positions of dominance – many European countries, including the UK, have recently begun to place more emphasis on the need for national competition authorities to enforce 'open' technological standards and to provide safeguards for all access points to the media.

Many countries also try to counteract concentrations of press ownership by subsidizing media organizations or media output that serve minorities or, more generally, that add to the diversity and range of 'voices' in the media. Some European countries provide direct subsidies to promote diversity in the print media (CE, 1996: 42–3). Sweden, for example, provides direct subsidies to newspapers that occupy a weak market position. In Norway too, financial support is available to less popular daily newspapers; support is also given to certain political, cultural and scientific magazines. In Belgium, the French-language press is supported by funds contributed by the broadcasting sector and a portion of commercial advertising revenues has been set aside each year to provide subsidies for the Flemish press. Several European countries do not provide grants for the press but a few offer subsidies for broadcast services targeted at specific minority groups. In the UK, for example, the Welsh-language television channel (S4C) relies heavily on a substantial public subsidy each year to make ends meet and public funds are also available through the Gaelic Television Committee to finance Gaelic-language programming broadcasts in Scotland.

Another method used in some parts of Europe to tackle concentrations of press ownership is to try to separate ownership from control. Some countries have adopted 'editorial agreements' which seek to prevent proprietors from influencing the editorial content of the media products that they own. The terms of such agreements between owners and editors vary and most are constituted on an informal or voluntary rather than a statutory basis.

Norway provides a good example. Here such a policy has been adopted since 1953 and for the most part it appears to have met with success in securing the independence of editors to take the lead on all editorial decisions free of interference from proprietors. The terms of Norway's declaration of *Rights and Duties of the Editor*, agreed by both editors and publishers, not only give the editor 'full freedom to shape the opinion of the paper' but also require him or her to 'promote an impartial and free exchange of information and opinion' and to 'strive for what he/she feels serves society'.[2]

Editorial interference by owners can often be indirect as well as direct. So, in order for editorial agreements to work effectively, they need to embrace a number of elements. It is essential that media owners be prevented from literally dictating, prescribing, rewriting or otherwise directly interfering in editorial matters. But media owners also need to be restrained from pestering or intimidating editors and journalists into adopting certain viewpoints or ignoring others. The issue of who has a say in the dismissal and replacement of editors or other key personnel is of crucial importance. An owner's power to threaten dismissal or to select new appointees who share a similar outlook can be used to reshape editorial policy without the need ever to interfere directly with content. Such powers can be used to establish an unhealthy culture of obedience and self-censorship. Additional powers may lie in an owner's control over all major managerial decisions (including, possibly, such issues as outsourcing of stories or consolidation or sharing of journalistic resources with other products).

The range of strategies through which a determined media proprietor can exert influence over the content of the products he or she owns is so extensive as to make it virtually impossible for any editorial agreement to fully guarantee the independence of editors and journalists. For this reason, editorial agreements do not entirely dispense with the need for diverse media ownership. Nonetheless, as is demonstrated by the experience of countries such as Norway, a carefully worded agreement backed up by the force of law can offer high levels of protection for editorial independence.

Another important source of support for pluralism across Europe comes in the form of each country's continued commitment to maintaining a national public service broadcasting entity. However promising the growth of new media may be, a market-led media economy dominated by commercial suppliers cannot be expected to give rise naturally to the open and diverse system of media provision which is essential for the preservation of pluralism. Policy interventions such as curbs on ownership, press subsidies and editorial agreements can and do help to reinforce diversity and pluralism within the commercial media sector in Europe. But, in addition, it is worth noting the extent to which publicly funded non-commercial broadcasting organizations who are wholly dedicated to the provision of a range and diversity of high-quality programming, as well as to accurate and impartial news coverage and to the principle of universal provision, also help to sustain media pluralism throughout Europe.

---

## Notes

1. According to information submitted to MM-CM in July 1997 by the national correspondent for France.

2. Citations from *Rights and Duties of the Editor*, signed 22 October 1953, revised in 1973, published by Association of Norwegian Editors.

# 10

# Towards a Harmonized EU Policy Initiative?

The quest to curb the development of excessive national and transnational media empires surfaced fairly persistently on the European policy agenda throughout the 1990s, but disappeared again each time amidst a welter of controversy. Newly emerging patterns of cross-sectoral domination in the communications and media industries of the 21st century – accommodated by regulatory change in several European member states – seem to provide an ever more compelling case for action at the EU level. But many influential industrial voices are firmly opposed to 'interference' from Europe in the design of media and cross-media ownership regulations. The legality of any European intervention aimed at curbing media concentrations to promote pluralism is open to question and there are many practical obstacles to harmonization of policy.

This chapter focuses on the Commission's efforts to work towards a pan-European initiative on media ownership. It examines the difficulties and conflicts experienced in trying to build up a consensus in favour of a new Directive in this area. Since, in the absence of any harmonizing legislation, European-level regulation of media concentrations remains purely a matter for competition interventions, the role played by DG4 (the Competition Directorate) in policing ownership of the media is considered below.

## Ownership policy and EU law: a question of competence?

The legal framework of the European Union is determined principally by the 1957 Treaty of Rome, and by amendments subsequently agreed in the 1986 Single European Act and the Treaty on European Union or

'Maastricht' Treaty (Weatherill and Beaumont, 1995: 1–41). The EU, operating under the auspices of the European Commission, may take action to create or harmonize European laws only if and when a remit for such action has been established through these treaties.

The general effect of the Single European Act and the Maastricht Treaty has been to adjust the institutional structure of the Community and to progressively expand its formal competencies beyond those agreed in the initial Treaty of Rome. Even so, there is little or no direct reference to the media or to policies for the media in any of these treaties (Goldberg et al., 1998: 152). Instead, European media policy – especially audiovisual policy – tends to be founded on broad EU objectives or more general articles within the treaties applied in the specific context of the media sector. For example, the 1989 EC Directive 'Television Without Frontiers', which was mainly concerned with establishing a single borderless market for any European television service, reflected aims set out in 1957 Treaty of Rome, such as the free exchange of services between member states.[1]

The competence of the European Commission to initiate policies concerning pluralism and media ownership is far from certain. The EU's general rules on competition apply to the media as to any other economic sector but, while serving to restrict dominant market positions or anti-competitive behaviour, these are not specifically designed to promote pluralism (Iosifides, 1996: 24). The Maastricht Treaty (Article 128) introduced competence for Community intervention in pursuit of cultural objectives, but this is limited to support measures and it explicitly excludes the possibility of harmonization of legislation (Weatherill and Beaumont, 1995: 477). So, although concerns about national and transnational media concentrations have been on the pan-European policy agenda, on and off, for some time, it seems that the European Commission does not have any clear remit to promote pluralism and diversity within the media.

The promotion of pluralism has traditionally been undertaken at member state level. But because each member state has established a different set of domestic media ownership regulations to safeguard pluralism, an alternative justification may be called upon for Community intervention. The EU's wider objectives involve eliminating possible obstructions to the single internal European market, i.e. obstructions to the free movement of goods, persons, services and capital.[2] Divergences in national media ownership legislation could, it has been argued, serve to obstruct the internal market by impeding cross-border investment in European media. So, quite separately from the issue of pluralism, this 'internal market' argument can be seen as providing the Commission with competence to tackle regulation of media ownership throughout the member states.

The European Parliament has also taken a close interest in media concentrations and, at various stages (e.g. in the February 1990 'Resolution on Media Takeovers and Mergers'), has called on the Commission to bring forward proposals aimed at harmonizing restrictions on media ownership and guaranteeing pluralism throughout Europe. According to Beltrame (1996: 4), the main protagonists for more effective measures to protect pluralism, both within Parliament and at the Commission, are Italian MEPs who are particularly concerned about the situation in their own country and especially the position of Fininvest. Moreover, Parliament's concerns have persistently been expressed in terms of the need for pluralism, and without any acknowledgement of limitations in the EU's competence in this area.

For its own part, the Commission took the first major step towards a pan-European policy approach to media ownership with the publication of a Green Paper on pluralism and media concentration (CEC, 1992). This document emerged as a response to the concerns expressed by Parliament about the need to safeguard pluralism but, at the same time, the Green Paper emphasized that the main justification for European-level intervention would be completion of the single market (an area where the Commission clearly has competence) rather than pluralism (which, at least officially, is supposed to be a matter for member states). This dichotomy, according to Hitchens (1994: 587), 'produces a tension which pervades the whole of the Green Paper'.

The 1992 Green Paper reviewed existing levels of media concentration in Europe and suggested three possible policy options: first, no action at the pan-European level; second, action to improve levels of transparency; or third, positive intervention – via a regulation or a Directive – to harmonize media ownership rules throughout the member states. But, almost a decade on from the publication of the 1992 Green Paper, no formal agreement has yet been reached on which of these options would best serve the needs of the European Union. So, by default, Option I appears to have taken the lead. The failure to move forward decisively on one or other of these options may be attributed, in large measure, to the range of conflicting opinions within Europe about what the aims and the substance of a collective policy on media ownership ought to be.

## Competing policy objectives: a dilemma for the Commission

The path towards a harmonized approach to media ownership policy became progressively more tortuous following the publication of the 1992

Green Paper because of diverging ideas about the goals such a policy ought to strive towards. In part, this reflected the fundamental question of whether the Commission has any legal right to pursue policies aimed at safeguarding pluralism (Beltrame, 1996; Hitchens, 1994). Parliament appeared to believe so and, throughout the early 1990s, was pressing for action to address the many worrying examples of concentrations which could readily be observed in national and transnational European media markets. The Council of Europe also evidently believes that pluralism is integral to the principle of freedom of speech and, as such, should be protected under the European legal order (Lange and Van Loon, 1991: 26). However, the 1992 Green Paper concluded that EU intervention in media ownership legislation may be justified only on the basis of securing the proper functioning of the internal market and *not* on the basis of protection of pluralism (CEC, 1992: 99).

Because concerns about competition and promoting the single market are different from concerns about pluralism, the implied reasons for harmonizing media ownership restrictions under these different approaches immediately diverge (Iosifides, 1996: 24). Safeguarding pluralism implies a need for European-wide restrictions which would eliminate undesirable concentrations of media power, whereas promoting competition implies equalization of ownership restrictions purely by reference to the economic needs of industry. Some mergers which do not threaten competition might pose a threat to plurality. Since media pluralism is a special concern in its own right, 'reliance on a competitive environment to foster pluralism may be to adopt a too simplistic approach' (Hitchens, 1994: 591).

From the outset, the Commission's approach to harmonization of media ownership was characterized by uncertainty about aims and means. Rifts were apparent even within the Commission, and, according to Beltrame (1996: 4), these particularly reflected rivalry between DG4, which is responsible for competition, and DG15, which is responsible for the Internal Market. After DG15 took charge of advancing a pan-European media ownership policy in 1993, the Commission attempted 'to inscribe Parliament's quest for pluralism in the logic of the Internal Market' (1996: 4).

But contention about the appropriate legal basis for intervention was not the only obstacle thrown into the Commission's path (Harcourt, 1996). The 1992 Green Paper set in motion a prolonged period of public consultation concerning which of the options set out at its conclusion would represent the best course of action. The responses to this consultation introduced an additional layer of complexity and contention to the issue of what objectives a harmonized European media ownership policy regime ought to be pursuing (Kaitatzi-Whitlock, 1996).

During the Commission's preliminary consultation, opinions were received from the Economic and Social Committee (ESC) and from the European Parliament, both of which came out in favour of Option III – i.e. action to harmonize national restrictions on ownership. The Fayot/ Schinzel Report (EP, 1994) on pluralism and media concentration was voted on at the European Parliament in January 1994 and received a majority of votes in favour. It urged the Commission to address the expansion of media conglomerates across European borders and cross-media ownership by introducing, as soon as possible, a new Directive on media ownership.

But, as well as these calls for more effective harmonized restrictions aimed at safeguarding pluralism, the Commission was also faced with a number of contradictory arguments favouring the introduction of a more liberalised pan-European policy regime. The views of individual European media firms themselves left a significant impression. Representations to the Commission were also received from industry federations and from specially commissioned reports such as that of the High Level or 'Bangemann' Group (Bangemann, 1994). Individual member states themselves tended to be rather noncommittal, at least initially, with formal positions taken up only after the interests of domestic industry groups could be established. This, perhaps, was one of the most telling signals to emerge from the European 'debate'.

The results of the first consultation phase after the 1992 Green Paper confirmed that positions were divided (CEC, 1994). Not surprisingly, it was Parliament, the ESC, journalists' federations and trade unions rather than industry who emphasized the protection of pluralism as a primary objective for Community action on media ownership rules. The Commission was in sympathy and asserted that 'the single market cannot be put into practice at the expense of pluralism' (1994: 7).

Industry participants also supported the need for action, but on a quite different and divergent agenda. The Commission summarized the industry's views thus: 'the current national rules on media ownership must change, in particular so as to cope with globalization and the impact of new technologies. On the other hand, the question of the level – national or European – at which change must occur is the subject of vague or divided positions' (1994: 13). Many media firms regarded the existing patchwork of media ownership rules across Europe as an impediment to investment – a position which the Commission endorsed – and they called for action to smooth the wide inconsistencies and disparities between current national media ownership rules.

The UK broadcaster ITV, for instance, lobbied extensively about a situation whereby, under domestic UK media ownership legislation, all

EU operators have equal rights of access to ownership of UK terrestrial broadcasting licences whereas, in some other EU member states, levels of access to ownership of broadcasting for non-nationals is more tightly restricted (Beltrame, 1996: 5). Domestic ownership restrictions in the early 1990s meant that ITV companies were obliged to remain relatively small and vulnerable to takeover while overseas expansion was obstructed by a complicated maze of non-reciprocal media ownership rules across Europe. So, according to ITV, it was difficult for UK broadcasters to achieve the critical mass needed to enhance their competitive position internationally and to take advantage of whatever additional economies were promised by new technology and the single market.

Similar concerns were expressed by operators in other countries. Italian media group L'Espresso, for example, agreed that disparities between national rules distorted the allocation of investments across Europe: 'car pénalisent les pays dans lesquelles les régimes juridiques concernant la propriété des médias sont plus rigides'[3] (Editoriale L'Espresso, 1993: 4).

Whether the goal motivating these expressions of concern about regulatory disparities was, simply, open and equal transnational competition within Europe might well be questioned. All such calls for change seemed to favour liberalization. The fear of losing competitiveness to 'foreign' rivals was deployed extensively and judiciously by companies (with a clear commercial self-interest in expansion) not only at the pan-European level but also, particularly, at the national level. Industrial calls for deregulation in EU member states such as Italy, France and Germany as well as the UK repeatedly emphasized the need to match the competitiveness of other European media rivals (MacLeod, 1996).

A persistent theme in industry submissions to the Commission was the effect of new technology and associated not-to-be-missed opportunities. UK media and publishing group Pearson suggested that 'Community action is required *now* to ensure that emerging forms of broadcasting are not distorted in their infancy'. Harmonization, according to Pearson, should 'take the form of a liberalization of the current regulatory environment – introducing the lightest regulatory regime consistent with maintaining the aim of diversity of media ownership' (1993: 1).

The European Federation of Magazine Publishers which represents the interests of European magazine publishers also argued that 'publishers should not be disadvantaged (by media or cross-ownership rules) from taking a full and in many cases a leading role in the development of multimedia trends in technology' (FAEP, 1993: 3). The European Publishers Council expressed its case in stronger language. Referring to the Fayot/Schinzel Motion, which stressed the need for measures to limit European media concentrations, the EPC warned that its recommendations would 'cripple the competitive ability of media companies in Europe' (1994: 1). Sir Frank Rogers, Chairman of the EPC, suggested that Europe 'could be left on a side road while American and Japanese media companies are freed to dominate the new global economies'.

In summary then, the results of the initial consultation exercise revealed widespread agreement about the need, in principle, for action to harmonize European media ownership legislation. But while some groups (especially the European Parliament) believed that the purpose of a harmonized regime should be to crack down on undesirable concentrations of media power that represent a threat to pluralism within Europe, others (especially industry participants in the larger member states) took the opposite view: that harmonization should aim to provide a more liberal media ownership regime, conducive to greater cross-border investment.

Such divergences of opinion between important interest groups made it difficult for the Commission to move forward. Conflicting objectives were highlighted when, for example, the follow-up Communication to the 1992 Green Paper spoke of 'facilitat(ing) the exercise of freedom of establishment for media companies and the free movement of media services in the Union, while maintaining pluralism in the face of certain concentrations' (CEC, 1994: 6). Contradictory policy agendas were also apparent in the contrast between objectives simultaneously being pursued in other Directorates of the Commission. While the drive towards a European 'Information Society' was characterized by the theme of 'liberalization' (espoused most notably by Commissioner Bangemann of DG13, the Directorate responsible for Telecoms, Information Industries and Innovation), this did not sit altogether comfortably with the wish to protect indigenous cultures and to accommodate safeguards for pluralism, expressed by DG15 (Schlesinger and Doyle, 1995).

So, rather than proceeding directly to formal proposals for a draft Directive in 1994, DG15 instead embarked on a second round of consultation and it circulated two specially commissioned studies – one looking at the criterion of actual audience as a way to measure media concentrations (GAH, 1994) and the other at the definition of a 'media controller' (Mounier and Robillard, 1994). But responses to this second round of consultation only appeared to reaffirm the lack of consensus between opposing ideological camps as to the aims of a harmonized European media ownership policy (CEC, 1997). Again, the European Parliament and the Economic and Social Committee confirmed their support for harmonization aimed at safeguarding pluralism. But, again, the majority of responses to the Commission came from large media firms expressing the view that harmonization ought to provide a more liberal media ownership regime, conducive to greater cross-border investment.

In addition, the Commission was faced with practical problems associated with the enormous discrepancies in national market sizes across Europe. An absolute ceiling on media ownership capable of preventing undesirable concentrations in smaller countries would clearly place a very tight leash on media companies operating in large markets. On the other hand, if thresholds were set by reference to a certain proportion or percentage of national audiences (say, at 10 per cent of the national media market), then operators in large member states would be allowed to grow considerably larger than rivals in smaller countries.

Such difficulties deterred most European member states from firmly supporting the need for a harmonized media ownership regime, and others (especially the UK) felt compelled to speak out in favour of the principle of subsidiarity. The UK's submission to DG15 pointed out that, even on the grounds of promoting the Internal Market, there was little to be gained from harmonizing media ownership rules, since the *main* obstructions to cross-border expansion by European media companies were cultural and linguistic barriers, not disparities in national regulations. This point was echoed by many industry players who were opposed to any involvement by the Commission in the determination of media ownership rules for Europe (Tucker, 1997).

But, quite apart from the potential for the status quo to disrupt the Commission's wider objectives of completing the Internal Market, a range of other arguments could be articulated in favour of action on media ownership at the European rather than the national level. The most compelling of these might be that dominant media operators in Europe wield such significant political power in their domestic markets as to impede national regulators from making pluralism the key priority in the design of media ownership policy (Humphreys, 1997: 9). Clearly, pan-European policy-makers cannot overlook the needs of industry. EU policy-making is not immune to industrial lobbying but, because of the diversity of national interests represented at the European level, there may arguably be less opportunity for any individual media player to superimpose its own requirements on the policy formulation process.

Against a background of increasing concerns about the competitiveness of domestic industries, the system of allegiances between national political parties and media industry participants, evident in many member states, has made it virtually impossible for national regulators in the large European markets to buck the general trend towards deregulation. Industrial participants in these markets are amongst the most vociferous opponents of a pan-European policy aimed at protecting pluralism (or, as some would have it, unnecessary 'Brussels bureaucracy'), and it is difficult to escape the conclusion that this reflects the potential dilution of their own influence at the pan-European level.

## Towards an EU Directive

### Draft proposals for a 'media pluralism' Directive (1996)

Despite the many obstacles to progress towards a pan-European media ownership policy, DG15 managed to take a step forward in autumn 1996 with the first draft of a possible EU Directive on media pluralism. The Commission's proposals involved a 30 per cent upper limit on monomedia ownership for radio and television broadcasters in their own transmission areas. In addition, the draft Directive suggested an upper limit for total media ownership – ownership of television, radio and/or newspapers – of 10 per cent of the market in which a supplier is operating. All market shares would be based on audience measures – i.e. calculated as a proportion of total television viewing, radio listenership or newspaper readership within the area in question – with consumption of each single type of media divided by one-third for the purposes of assessing a supplier's overall share of the total market. The proposed derogations would allow member states to exclude public service broadcasters from these upper limits, if they so wished.

The definition of precise upper limits for media ownership moved the policy debate onto a more practical footing. Inevitably, it also provided the site for major controversies about what level of diversity of ownership was appropriate for markets of different sizes. The approach taken in DG15's proposals for a draft Directive was to set the same fixed limits which would apply in any member state and either at the local, regional or national level, depending on which constituted the appropriate market for the media supplier in question. Crucially, the Commission took the view that what counts is market share within the specific transmission area for a broadcasting service. This contrasted with the approach taken, say in the UK, where what counts is a broadcaster's share of the national market, irrespective of what areas its service is transmitting in. From the point of view of achieving equality of pluralism for all European media consumers, the Commission's approach seemed highly effective. The problem was that it seems to disregard the fact that different market sizes – whether national or sub-national – can support different levels of diversity of ownership.

In principle, the imposition of a 30 per cent upper limit on monomedia radio, television or newspaper ownership plus a 10 per cent upper limit on total media ownership, does not seem unreasonable. If pluralism is to exist, then a minimum of four suppliers each in the radio, television and newspaper sectors or ten different suppliers in the market as a whole may seem an appropriate requirement. In practice, however, because of different rules and differing levels of resources available for media provision in each country, some of the member states of Europe immediately fell foul of these proposals, even in terms of diversity of ownership at the *national* level. For example, some smaller European countries had only two national broadcasters in 1996, each with a market share in excess of 30 per cent (Barnard et al., 1996). The number of observable transgressions throughout Europe multiplied as the focus shifted down to smaller regional and local levels. At the same time, the proposed upper monomedia ownership limit of 30 per cent paved the way for even higher levels of concentration in some larger national markets than was currently allowed.

DG15's proposals addressed the problem of diverging national regulations and they also seemed well suited to the task of establishing and protecting minimum levels of pluralism, in equal measure, for all citizens of the EU. But opponents of a pan-European policy initiative were quick to seize on the distinction between promoting pluralism and completing the Internal Market, and to question which of these objectives DG15's proposals were really aimed at. The Corporate Affairs Director of one of the UK's largest media firms expressed the following views on the 1996 draft Directive:

> You have to keep saying to them [the Commission], where is the problem? And they say 'single market' – they need to tidy up disparities. But they are *not* looking at it as a single market; they are talking about pluralism and diversity and saying they have competence in this area. Then, it's not a single market issue. Is it about tidying up the rules to increase cross-border sales or about preventing one person from owning too much? These are two completely different things. And they have tried to address both in one single document and they have fallen over themselves really, really badly . . .

Whether member states wanted and could afford to resource equal levels of diversity of ownership at the sub-national as well as national level was an additional matter. It was not at all clear how member states or the EU at large would find the economic means to redress shortfalls in diversity of ownership in some sub-national or smaller national markets.

DG15's response to objections raised (in particular from the UK and Germany) was to promise a more flexible approach to the upper ceilings suggested in the July 1996 draft, indicating that the 30 per cent thresholds could be varied if national circumstances so demanded. But the Commission's negotiating position on upper ceilings was constrained by Parliament's consistent support for robust measures to counteract concentrations. Clearly, the greater the discretionary power left to member states in setting their own upper limits on media and cross-media owner-ship, the less effective any new directive would be, whatever its objectives.

### Draft proposals for a 'media ownership' directive (1997)

A revised set of proposals put forward by DG15 in spring 1997 introduced two small but significant modifications (Gabara, 1997). First, the title of the proposed Directive was changed from 'Concentrations and Pluralism' to 'Media Ownership' in the Internal Market. This signalled a move to deflect the focus from pluralism (where the Commission's competence would be in question) towards the aim of removing obstacles to the Internal Market.

Second, a 'flexibility clause' was introduced. This added, to the proposed derogations, the flexibility for individual member states to exclude any broadcaster they wished from the (unchanged) upper limits, provided that the broadcaster in question was not simultaneously infringing these upper thresholds in more than one member state, and provided that other 'appropriate measures' were used to secure pluralism. 'Appropriate measures' might include establishing, within any organization that breached the limits, 'windows for independent programme suppliers' or a 'representative programming committee' (CEC, 1997).

These modifications represented an unambiguous withdrawal from the original ambition of imposing a fixed minimum level of diversity of ownership for all European markets. Instead, member states could decide for themselves (at least in the short term) whether or not the ownership thresholds set out in the Directive should apply to organizations operating within their own national territories. According to the revised proposals, there would be no absolute requirement for member states to enforce the upper thresholds set out in the Directive, but the new measures would prevent any member state from adopting *more* restrictive domestic media ownership rules (which, arguably, could obstruct cross-border investment or distort competition).

In effect then, as the switch of title suggested, the Directive was no longer about guaranteeing an equal right to pluralism (as represented by diversity of media ownership) for all EU citizens, irrespective of which European markets they happened to live in. Although, in theory, the proposed Directive introduced a uniform set of media ownership restrictions throughout the EU, in practice, the 'flexibility clause' would allow member states to maintain whatever upper restrictions on ownership were affordable – either economically or politically – in their own territories. What, then, was the point of introducing a harmonizing initiative?

Such back-tracking was intended to boost support for a new Directive but, at the same time, it made it difficult to see how a harmonized approach could appease long-standing concerns (especially in the European Parliament) about national and transnational concentrations of media ownership in Europe. And, in spite of this 'legalistic subterfuge', opposition to the idea of any pan-European policy initiative was not extinguished (Gabara, 1997). The problem remained that *regional* media suppliers (e.g. the UK broadcaster, ITV), whose local market share exceeded 30 per cent but whose share of the national market was relatively small, were to be caught out by the proposed European-wide rules in exactly the same way as what are perceived as genuine 'media moguls'; i.e. *national* media suppliers whose market share exceeded 30 per cent (e.g. Fininvest in Italy, or TF1 in France, or News International in the UK). But if member states used the 'flexibility clause' to exempt domestic operators from the proposed upper thresholds, then the new Directive would be meaningless. For some commentators, the legal uncertainty which the exemption clause would create 'would be worse than not having a common Directive at all. In the absence of an EU law, potential investors at least have the certainty that the national legislation applies' (Gabara, 1997).

Debate about the revised EU initiative had to be postponed in March 1997 'in the face of ferocious lobbying against it' (Tucker, 1997). The European Publishers Council again publicly expressed its view that a pan-European media ownership initiative was unnecessary and would only hinder the development of European media companies (McEvoy, 1997; Tucker, 1997). ITV also voiced strong concern that the UK's regional television system could be jeopardized under the new draft Directive, unless a 'cast-iron guarantee' of exemption were given to regional broadcasters (ITVA, 1997).

A uniform set of media ownership restrictions imposed rigidly throughout all European markets seemed unfeasible, both economically and politically. But, if the solution was to adopt a flexible approach, then it was open to question whether the Commission should get involved at all, given that member states themselves were better placed than DG15 to take account of and directly legislate for the particular characteristics of their own markets. If a Directive on media ownership was to convey any useful benefits over and above the status quo, something more visionary than a 'flexible' approach was needed.

One possible solution for the Commission might have been to acknowledge that a uniform set of media ownership rules was unworkable because the resources available for media provision are unevenly spread across EU media markets. If a redistribution of resources was out of the question, then a non-uniform set of rules offered the only realistic option.

For example, a 'tiered' approach – stipulating required levels of diversity of ownership for markets of different sizes – might have offered some advantages over the proposed 'flexible' approach. First, a 'tiered' approach would remove much of the uncertainty (for cross-border investment) associated with widely divergent national systems of media ownership regulation. Second, it self-evidently takes account of the problem posed by divergences in the resources available for media provision in markets of different sizes. Third, it might help to transcend the problem of dominant national suppliers exerting undue influence over domestic political mechanisms designed to curb their growth.

However, any such alternatives would have received little or no support from large media players who continued to lobby against the introduction of an EU initiative. Throughout the late 1990s, DG15 found itself unable to build a supporting consensus around any proposals for a new Directive on media ownership. What emerges clearly is that, at the collective European as well as at the national level, the perceived economic opportunity costs of restricting indigenous media firms have completely overshadowed concerns about safeguarding pluralism. So, the 'patchwork' of regulations determined at national level – and, increasingly, determined in response to industrial or economic concerns – has survived into a new millennium and there seems little chance that DG15 will be able to take action to replace it any time in the near future.

### Farewell pluralism; long live competition policy!

If harmonized rules on media and cross-media ownership now seem highly unlikely, the Commission still retains some interest in regulating concentrations in the media industry. The EU's general rules on competition apply to the media as to any other economic sector and DG4, the Directorate responsible for competition, has intervened on several occasions to deal with proposed mergers or allegations of anti-competitive conduct involving large European media players. Of course, while European competition law serves to restrict dominant market positions or anti-competitive behaviour, it is not specifically designed to encourage or safeguard pluralism. Even so, competition-based interventions have played a valuable role in helping to promote diversity and pluralism within European media and communications industries in recent years.

The EU's general rules on competition, contained in Articles 85, 86 and 90 of the European Union Treaty and in the 1989 Merger Control Regulation, are intended to ensure the efficient operation of markets and to prevent excessive dominance or abuses of market power. Article 85 focuses on restrictive practices and prevents private-sector companies from entering agreements that are anti-competitive in their effects. Similarly, Article 86 prohibits any abuse of a dominant position by commercial firms within the Internal Market, i.e. behaviour of an exploitative nature such as overcharging. Article 90 extends these prohibitions to organizations operating in the public sector. In order to enforce these articles, DG4 has authority to investigate instances of concentrated ownership and, if anti-competitive behaviour is found, to require that divestitures are made or seek other remedies.

DG4 is also responsible for examining any mergers or acquisitions that fall under the terms of what is called the Merger Control Regulation. The Merger Control Regulation, which was adopted in December 1989 and came into force in September 1990, introduced a new framework explicitly devoted to dealing with mergers (Weatherill and Beaumont, 1995: 811). The 1989 Regulation gives the Commission pre-emptive powers to stop concentrations of ownership from occurring in any industrial sector when the outcome might be a distortion of competition. Under the terms of the Regulation, proposed mergers or acquisitions that would result in an entity with a combined worldwide turnover in excess of ECU 5 billion must be notified to DG4 in advance. DG4 then decides whether the proposed merger is likely to create a dominant position and rules on whether or not it may go ahead.

DG4 has used its powers to review and, in some cases, to block proposed mergers and joint ventures involving media and communications players. For example, in 1994 the Commission took the decision to stop a proposed joint venture in Germany between media giants Bertelsmann and Kirch and former state telecommunications operator Deutsche Telekom. The new venture would have created MSG digital services group – according to some, 'a classic gatekeeper case with undue power' (Hirsch and Petersen, 1998: 215). DG4 took the view that this alliance would give MSG an excessively dominant position in the pay-TV market in Germany and so it ruled against allowing the deal to go ahead.

In 1998, the Commission intervened once again to prevent a very similar merger involving Kirch, Bertelsmann and Deutsche Telecom which would have given these players an extremely dominant position in digital pay-TV in Germany. One of the Commission's main concerns was 'that a company with control over the bulk of programmes and the technology needed to watch and distribute them would hold too strong a position in an emerging market' (D. Hargreaves, 2000a: 21).

Since then, a number of additional cases of proposed diagonal and vertical mergers involving media content suppliers and communications infrastructure operators have come before the European competition authorities. The Commissioner at DG4 as at 2001, Mario Monti, also happened to be in charge of DG15 from 1995 to 1999 when that Directorate was most active in attempting to frame a possible Directive on media ownership. So Commissioner Monti, having moved to DG4, has again found himself at the centre of conflicting opinions about what role the Commission ought to play in encouraging or curbing major concentrations of ownership in the rapidly changing environment of media and communications of the 21st century.

The proposed merger between media conglomerate Time Warner and America Online (AOL), notified to the Commission in spring 2000, once again presented DG4 with the question of how best to deal with vertical concentrations in the communications sector, i.e. combinations of both content and carriage. The AOL/Time Warner deal attracted similar concerns from competition authorities in the USA where Time Warner was a major player in content provision across several sectors of the media and AOL was the largest Internet service provider. The main worries, both in Brussels and Washington, were that the combined group could damage rivals in content provision by restricting access to AOL's distribution infrastructure or it could harm rivals in infrastructure provision by denying them access to Time Warner's content.

Because of its novelty and scale, the AOL/Time Warner deal was seen, in some ways, as an important test case of how regulators would deal with vertical mergers in the communications sector. Some of the complexities surrounding regulation of monopolies in times of technological change were discussed in Chapter 3. One of the main challenges is judging how best to balance the need for competition (i.e. by safeguarding market access) against the need to encourage investment in new services and infrastructure (i.e. by allowing investors a sufficient opportunity to reap profits). In the case of AOL/Time Warner, regulators on both sides of the Atlantic were especially concerned that an alliance between AOL and such a significant content provider as Time Warner might stifle competition in the growing market for high-speed Internet access. But the proposed AOL/Time Warner deal also highlighted the more general problem that regulators do not know how exactly new communications technologies will develop and, in turn, what impact mergers involving 'old' and 'new' media players may eventually have on rivals and on consumers' welfare (D. Hargreaves et al., 2000a: 22).

Mergers of this sort clearly do have implications for pluralism. As discussed earlier, monopolized control over bottlenecks (such as content, or facilities or access points), especially when combined with strategies of vertical integration, can give individual players very significant degrees of influence over rivals and over what sorts of services and content are made available to the public. But imposing ownership restraints might serve to inhibit investment in the development of new media and communication markets. By contrast, the competition-based approach of ensuring open access for rivals and of preventing abusive behaviour provides policy instruments that are flexible and that generally seem better suited to the task of regulating vertical mergers and preventing bottlenecks across the converging media and communications sectors.

DG4 has not been timid about requesting concessions or even blocking deals involving leading media and communications players where there have been concerns about excessive dominance or the potential for abuses of market power. For example, in June 2000 it prohibited Worldcom's proposed takeover of telecommunications rival Sprint on the basis that it would lead to excessive dominance in the communications sector. The Commission also took a stand in 2000 against Time Warner's separate proposed $20 billion acquisition of UK music group EMI on the basis that that this would create an oligopoly in the music market with undesirable implications for consumers (D. Hargreaves et al. 2000a: 22). In the same year, the proposed AOL/Time Warner merger was granted approval by the relevant authorities on both sides of the Atlantic, but only on condition that rivals be allowed access, on fair and equal terms, to the merged company's main distribution platforms.

The approach of requiring monopolists or dominant players to give third-party access to rivals on terms that are fair and non-discriminatory has increasingly been adopted by European competition authorities and, as discussed earlier, is based on the so-called 'essential facility' doctrine pioneered in the US. It was exemplified in another deal recently scrutinized by DG4 when French media company Vivendi, which owned 49 per cent of Canal Plus, proposed merging with Seagram, owner of Universal film studios. The resulting company, Vivendi Universal, would be 'a Franco-Canadian entertainment and communications powerhouse' expected to rival AOL/Time Warner (Buckley and Iskander, 2000: 22). The merger was approved by DG4 in October 2000, but only on the basis of a 'package of undertakings that would address Commission worries about the merged group's power in the pay-TV markets in France, Belgium, Spain, Italy, the Netherlands and the Nordic countries' (D. Hargreaves et al., 2000b: 23). This included Vivendi's agreement to dispose of a major investment stake in UK pay-TV operator BSkyB acquired the previous year. The main concession required of the group was an undertaking to provide third-party access on fair terms for Canal Plus' rivals to Universal's films, at least for the next five years.

The Commission's recent competition-based interventions in the media and communications industries have undoubtedly served to encourage wider market access and to promote greater diversity and pluralism. The useful role played by competition law in safeguarding against abuses of excessive market power across the converging media and communications sectors has led some, particularly large industry players, to ask whether regulation of media ownership can now be left entirely to competition law.

The promotion of competition in the media sector is clearly a vital starting point for ensuring pluralism. But there are two main problems with relying solely on competition law. First, it is not particularly effective at national level in some European countries (Goldberg et al., 1998: 18) and, at the collective EU level, it is evident that many media mergers and alliances are also ignored by DG4 because they fall below the revenue thresholds set out in the 1989 Merger Control Regulation. So it is questionable whether existing competition laws in Europe are sufficiently well attuned to pick up on all significant media mergers and acquisitions or whether, without additional sector-specific regulations, many would fall through the regulatory loop.

Second, safeguarding competition and promoting pluralism are different objectives. The need to ensure plurality in the media on democratic, social and cultural grounds is a separate and distinct policy objective from ensuring market efficiency through competition. As acknowledged in recent UK White Paper on communications, '[a] competitive market is likely to be one with many voices and diverse content, though there is no guarantee that this will be the case' (DTI/DCMS, 2000: 36). Sometimes, media markets that raise no concerns in terms of competition may nonetheless lack the range and diversity of voices needed to safeguard pluralism.

Diversity and pluralism in the media cannot be ensured by competition policy alone. But nor indeed can they be guaranteed by any single policy instrument. As discussed in Chapter 2 above, media pluralism is determined by a number of factors. A strong competition policy provides a good basis for promoting diversity but additional policy instruments – sector-specific rules on media ownership, regulations to promote diverse content, etc. – also have a crucial and irreplaceable role to play in sustaining open and pluralistic media.

## Notes

1. Articles 59–66.

2. Free movement of capital is governed by Articles 67–73 of the Treaty of Rome and Articles 73b and 73g of the Treaty on European Union.

3. 'by penalizing those countries where the legal regime concerning media ownership is more strict.'

# 11

# Conclusions

## Ownership of the media matters

Questions surrounding who owns the media, and how much of it they are allowed to own, are important. But why these issues matter depends on the perspective from which they are approached. Decisions about whether and how to regulate ownership of the media call for reflection on what the consequences of concentrated media ownership might be, and *for whom*. Fundamental political questions arise as to whose interests a policy in this area ought to favour, and which regulatory design will best serve those interests.

Many writers have focused attention on the fact that ownership of the media matters to individual citizens or consumers and to *society* at large. It matters to society because a number of potential harms may result from concentrated media ownership, including the abuse of political power by media owners or the under-representation of some viewpoints. As suggested by Sánchez-Tabernero, '[l]e type d'influence que la concentration des médias exerce sur la société et le public déterminera les décisions politiques à adopter' (1993: 189). Citizens and voters have need of access to a variety of political viewpoints (Cavallin in Picard, 2000: 162). Individuals expect and need a system of media provision that supplies a wide range of ideas, viewpoints and different forms of cultural expression.

Recognition of society's need for 'pluralism' and of the threat to pluralism posed by media concentrations has, historically, provided the main impetus for regulating ownership of the media. As discussed in Part I, one of the main concerns surrounding concentrations of media ownership is the risk for democracy and for the wider political system when individual 'voices' gain excessive control over the media. Democracy is threatened if individual media owners, with the power to propagate a single political viewpoint, are allowed to predominate over the supply of media. Cultural pluralism is another important concern. Cultural diversity and the cohesiveness of society will be threatened unless the cultures, views and values of all groupings within society (such as those sharing a particular language, race or creed) are reflected within the media.

So, diversity of ownership of the media is generally seen as one of the essential conditions for sustaining political and cultural pluralism. Pluralism is a key social objective but it is not the only reason why ownership of the media matters. It also matters because it affects the way in which the media industry is able to manage the resources available for media provision. The economic and financial performance of the industry is, at least partly, dependent on the market structures in which media firms operate and on media ownership configurations. Restrictions on ownership could, for example, result in replication of resources which prevents the industry from capitalizing on all potential economies of scale. So, media ownership policy matters to society because of the economic costs or benefits that result from preventing or encouraging concentrations of media ownership.

The issue of economic performance is not solely a matter for broad societal interest, but is obviously of immense concern to *media firms*. In general, the level of earnings and profits that media enterprises are able to generate will depend, to some extent at least, on what sort of corporate configurations they are allowed to adopt. So a second constituency that is highly concerned with questions surrounding media ownership regulation is media owners. But when considering what approach to ownership regulation will enable firms to arrive at 'optimal' corporate configurations, a distinction needs to be drawn between, on one hand, strategies of expansion that advance the efficiency of firms and thus the wider economic welfare of society and, on the other hand, expansion strategies that only advance the private interests of particular media firms or their managers or shareholders.

Arguments based around 'economic' concerns have gained increased status in debates about media ownership policy in recent years. To respond to these concerns appropriately, it is important to investigate what, if any, economic benefits or costs may be associated with enlarged and diversified media firms. One of the worrying conclusions that emerges from studying recent changes in media ownership policy in the UK and across Europe is that relatively little independent investigation or systematic analysis of the consequences of these changes has been carried out by policy-makers. The ideology underlying media ownership policy appears to have shifted quite significantly since the early 1990s, but without much effort to subject the grounds for this shift to critical examination.

This leads inexorably towards a third category of interests that are particularly affected by media ownership; namely, those of *politicians*. As many previous writers have suggested, the issue of who owns and controls the media, and how much they are allowed to own, matters to politicians. It matters because, as is exemplified with increasing clarity over time, those who control popular media have the power to make or break political reputations and careers.

As discussed in Part III, the conduct of media ownership policy changes in the UK in the 1990s indicates the extent to which narrow political objectives (rather than public interest concerns of any kind) can shape the agenda and outcome. Of course, problems arising from alignments between political and corporate media interests are by no means confined to the UK. A similar pattern of deregulation of media ownership, with policy-makers bending to the wishes of powerful and ambitious media groups, can be found in several other European countries. And across Europe, the redesign of ownership policies has taken place without much in the way of objective investigation or rigorous research into the economic consequences or the implications for pluralism.

The general absence of any robust body of independent research into the economic implications of deregulating media ownership has greatly favoured corporate interests. It has meant that, in general, large media firms' own interpretations of technological and market developments, and of the economic implications of these developments, have been allowed to dominate the policy agenda in the UK as elsewhere in Europe without any attempt at systematic empirical corroboration. As one senior UK policy-maker cited earlier put it:

What can I say? These were *political* decisions at root . . .

## Media are especially vulnerable to concentrations

The economics of monomedia and cross-media ownership and expansion were examined in Part II. The main conclusions which emerge are that television, radio or newspaper firms with a large monomedia (i.e. in one sector only) market share will enjoy a range of advantages. Confirming what is generally suggested by industrial economic theory, the positive relationship between market share and economic efficiency of media firms reflects the widespread availability of economies of scale in the media industry.

A crucial issue for monomedia firms operating in any of these media sectors is the extent to which their output is heterogeneous. The structure and extent of a firm's total costs are affected not only by its share of the market but also by the composition of that market share, in terms of how many different or similar products this represents. Single product media firms tend to enjoy significant scale economies as consumption (audiences or readership) of their product expands. Multi-product firms (such as EMAP with its 19 local radio stations, or News International, with its four national newspaper titles) reap the benefit of both economies of scale and economies of scope, but the latter will vary, depending on what level of resources is shared by 'rival' products held in common ownership.

Common ownership is not, in all cases, the only route to deriving economies in the media industry. The evidence discussed in Chapter 4 shows that, for broadcasters and newspaper publishers alike, rival owners may find it possible to share costs (e.g. components of media content, or support services) through agreements to co-operate with each other. Some differences of opinion exist about where exactly the line should be drawn on sharing costs with competing media suppliers and, of course, the need for individual products to sustain a unique brand identity naturally precludes some forms of cost-sharing (even when 'rival' products are held in common ownership).

In addition, rivalry about the terms for cost-sharing may impede shared use of duplicated resources between separate owners, even where this would obviously confer significant mutual benefits. The Finance Director of a major UK television company (cited earlier) refers to an example of this problem within the ITV network of regional broadcasters:

> Everyone [in ITV] is saying 'Can't we have one transmission centre and can't it be mine?' It's the classic ITV situation where everyone can see that basically its a good idea but nobody wants someone else to win so everybody ends up losing.

In a situation reminiscent of the problems which give rise to 'non-cooperative equilibrium', all suppliers are left worse off because each firm's desire to maximize its own individual gains defeats the opportunity for joint profit maximization. So, concentrated monomedia ownership remains the key to many cost-efficiencies in the radio, television and newspaper sectors.

Previous theorizing in industrial economics has drawn attention to the tendency towards concentration in any industry characterized by economies of scale. Clearly, media are no exception. Because of the presence of economies of scale and scope, and because size or 'critical mass' tends to confer other important advantages (e.g. negotiating power over advertisers, improved access to capital), there has always been a strong incentive for broadcasters or newspaper firms to seek to increase their share of respective markets. Consequently, the industry is particularly vulnerable to concentrations of monomedia ownership.

The industry is also prone to concentrations of cross-media ownership, but whether strategies of cross-media expansion may be attributable to economic motives is, in at least some cases, questionable. Whereas it is clear that a supplier operating in any *one or other* of the television broadcasting, radio broadcasting or newspaper publishing sectors may find ways of reducing costs (per unit of consumption of output) and improving its general economic efficiency as its overall share of the market expands, this may not always hold true in the case of diagonal expansion into other media product markets.

Many combinations of diagonal cross-media ownership undoubtedly give rise to significant cost-savings and economic efficiency gains for media owners. For example, combinations of print and electronic publishing create obvious synergies through opportunities for re-use of text and graphic content. Likewise, joint provision of telecommunications and television broadcasting will create economies by facilitating greater usage of the same distribution infrastructure. The spread of common digital technologies across different media and communication sectors is gradually increasing opportunities for shared exploitation of assets and resources across additional cross-sectoral combinations. But, when it comes to cross-ownership across the traditional sectors of the media – broadcasting and newspapers – there is little evidence that technological convergence has arrived yet and not much sign that such combinations of cross-ownership give rise to any significant economic efficiency gains.

The experience of UK media firms suggests that relatively few opportunities to make better use of collective resources will arise as a direct result of cross-ownership between the radio, television and newspaper sectors. Because distribution techniques tend to be entirely different in these sectors, common ownership would not yield any of the economic efficiencies available, say, in diagonal integration between a cable television and a telephony supplier. Production techniques are also different for radio, television and newspapers so, unless there happens to be an especially strong common content specialism, there will be few opportunities for economizing through transplanting or 'repurposing' of content.

However, individual media firms may themselves derive some commercial or strategic benefits from cross-ownership across traditional sectors of the media. Risk reduction may be the incentive for diagonal expansion. For example, newspaper publishers in the UK stand to benefit from diversifying out of their own relatively mature sector into the faster growth areas of commercial radio or television broadcasting. Highly cash-generative television broadcasters may choose to cross-invest in newspapers because there is a lower perceived risk in diversifying within than outside the media industry.

The opportunity to cross-promote existing products is another acknowledged advantage of media cross-ownership. As with risk-reduction strategies, the sorts of benefits which accrue to the firm as a result of the opportunity for cross-promotion have less to do with increased efficiency *per se*, than with maintaining and increasing individual firms' market power or dominance. The experience of UK media firms considered in Part II suggests that diagonal expansion may, in some cases, reflect individual managerial utility functions – i.e. the personal benefits or gratification achieved by managers of the media as a consequence of conglomerate expansion. In the UK media industry, the avoidance of a hostile takeover bid is commonly perceived to be a significant managerial incentive for diagonal expansion.

The crucial point, as far as policy-making is concerned, is that such benefits as arise from cross-ownership across traditional sectors of the media tend *not* to involve improved use of the limited resources available for the provision of media output, or any other economic gains which recognisably favour the interests of consumers or society at large. Instead, benefits tend to be of a corporate nature, primarily favouring the private interests of shareholders in specific media firms or, in some cases, managers of these firms.

This distinction between, on the one hand, the private interests of the owners and managers of commercial firms and, on the other hand, the wider economic interest is important. The two do not always overlap and it is the latter – society's interest in achieving the most efficient possible usage of resources – which is, or ought to be, the main concern for public policy.

## Systemic problems with existing mechanisms for curbing ownership

> ... It would be idle to pretend that we instituted properly rigorous scientific/economic analysis specifically to buttress our policy conclusions ... This is too political a market to regulate primarily because of economic objectives.

The words of this senior UK policy-maker involved in 'shepherding through' the media ownership policy changes in the 1996 Broadcasting Act point directly to a problem with the mechanism by which concentrations of media ownership are supposed to be regulated. In theory, curbs on concentrated media ownership safeguard democracy by protecting against unhealthy alignments of corporate media power and political power. But in practice, the pre-existence of these alignments serves to impede the instigation of such curbs.

Connections between the machinery of Government and the wider political system are, of course, unavoidable and exist in every country throughout Europe, as elsewhere. Sectional interests in the media are an important component of this wider system. Because politicians are increasingly driven by the desire to accommodate the wishes and aims of influential media groups, the extent to which competing public interest goals for media ownership regulation (of any sort) can make any impression on policy decisions is diminishing.

Precisely because media ownership is 'a difficult political minefield', the design of a regulatory scheme to deal with concentrations ought to be robust, equitable and squarely aimed at legitimate public policy objectives. Instead, the redesign of media ownership policies across Europe in recent years seems to have been uneven, unstable and aimed at accommodating particular corporate interests. The unavoidable conclusion is that the systems through which curbs on concentrated media power are decided in the UK and across Europe are in serious need of reform.

However, there is little or no prospect of this 'problem' gaining widespread recognition. Inasmuch as media interests have had the political power to re-design media ownership policies to their own ends, they have also been uniquely well placed to sustain a climate of public indifference to any negative consequences arising from these changes. It seems that a continuation of alignments between corporate media and political interests suits all of those who are empowered to instigate change. So the 'problem' rarely surfaces in channels likely to bring it to public attention – namely, media or political discourse. In the UK, for example, the very latest plans to 'reform' media ownership rules seem to be centred around dismantling, as quickly as possible, what few measures remain to hold in check the expansion of domestic media firms.

## Media ownership regulation in the future

Deficiencies in the system through which decisions on media ownership policy are taken will not easily be overcome. It strikes at the very heart of democracy when politicians and public servants choose to formulate policy in pursuit of objectives other than the public interest. But, since the media perform an increasingly influential role in political destinies, it is difficult to see how the problem of alignments between corporate media and political interests can be reversed. Democracy is subverted when changes in public policy are aimed at accommodating the interests of an elite, corporate media or otherwise, but it would also be diminished if responsibility for the determination of public policy were removed from elected public representatives.

One potential solution to this situation is the possibility that, at some stage in the future, regulation of media ownership will become unnecessary. As barriers to market entry diminish and as more and more new avenues for distribution of media become available, it is suggested that a diversity of political and cultural representations will flourish without any need for special ownership restrictions. At some stage in the future, diversity and pluralism may be sufficiently guaranteed by the continued proliferation of new outlets for media.

Whilst this viewpoint will gain ground as technological changes widen product choice, it cannot be said that pluralism is as yet a 'natural' feature of the markets for mass media. In 2001, the dominant media in the UK remain terrestrial analogue television channels (of which there are five) and national newspapers (12 daily titles) and well over 60 per cent of the latter market is controlled by just two commercial players. The advent of cable, satellite and the rapid growth of digital broadcasting and the Internet are all adding to diversity of media provision but, even with these 'new media', concerns about the impact on pluralism of concentrated ownership remain as poignant as ever.

The notion that the only justification for special rules on ownership of the media has been scarcity is, as Hitchens has suggested, a 'fallacy' (1995: 635). Restrictions on media and cross-media ownership are there to encourage diversity but, most especially, they are to do with avoiding an unhealthy domination of the media by individual owners. The economic and commercial incentives that encourage concentrations of ownership apply just as strongly to new as to traditional media. Indeed, many of the main players in digital broadcasting and online media provision are large well-established media conglomerates such as Time Warner and Bertelsmann who have moved speedily to secure their positions within newly developing technologies.

The future is unlikely to see the eliminatation of fundamental concerns about concentrated media power. Indeed, the growth of 'new' media and the Internet have been catalysts for a great many 'mega-mergers' and alliances involving large-scale media and communications corporations over recent years. Several of these deals – for example, the AOL/Time Warner merger or the acquisition of Endemol by Telefónica, both in 2000 – have underlined the perceived importance of developing market power across all major stages in the vertical supply chain. These emerging ownership configurations raise new concerns about bottlenecks and gateway monopolies in the media, with the associated implications for pluralism.

Control over key access points to the media, especially when combined with strategies of vertical integration, can give individual media players extremely high levels of influence over rivals and over what sorts of content and services are supplied to the public. Traditional media ownership regulations are, by and large, simply not attuned to tackling these problems. So European regulatory authorities have drawn increasingly on alternative policy instruments based on competition law to deal with them. For example, bottlenecks have been tackled by placing a duty on monopolists and dominant players to facilitate market access for rivals on fair and equal terms. And regulation of technical standards (to encourage the interoperability of rival systems) has been used to promote more open market access.

As patterns of concentrated media ownership and market power shift, competition-based interventions will undoubtedly play an important and positive role in helping to promote open markets and diversity. However, regulation of ownership based on competition concerns alone is not a sufficient means of ensuring pluralism. Sometimes, markets that raise no concerns in terms of competition may nonetheless lack the range and diversity of independent voices needed to safeguard pluralism. So, although promoting competition sometimes overlaps with promoting pluralism, these are fundamentally different objectives.

To maintain pluralism and avoid the risk of an unhealthy domination of the media by individual players, policy instruments other than competition law must come into play. Measures such as regulations to encourage diverse content, or special editorial agreements, or support measures for public service broadcasters all have a useful role to play in promoting pluralism and counteracting media concentrations. Above all, effective and equitable upper restraints on ownership are vitally important tools that no responsible democracy can afford to relinquish. Curbs on ownership provide a direct means of preventing harmful concentrations of media power and, as such, are indispensable safeguards for pluralism and democracy.

Given the proven dangers of ignoring concentrations of media power, the persistent march towards complete liberalization of national media ownership policies across Europe in recent years is a profound cause for concern. The broader question to be answered now is how can the conditions be created which would introduce democracy, and questions about how this can be ensured, as a meaningful issue in contemporary political and media discourse?

# References

Albarran, A. and Dimmick, J. (1996) 'Concentration and economies of multiformity in the communications industries', *Journal of Media Economics*, 9 (4): 41–50.

Alexander A, Owers, J. and Carveth, R. (eds) (1998) *Media Economics: Theory and Practice*, 2nd edn, Muhwah, NJ: Lawrence Erlbaum Associates.

Associated Newspapers (2001) *Communications White Paper Consultation: Comments by Associated Newspapers Ltd*, February. Posted under 'Responses to the White Paper' at http://www.communicationswhitepaper.gov.uk/

Bagdikian, B. (1992) *The Media Monopoly*, 4th edn, Boston, MA: Beacon Press.

Bangemann, M. (Chairman) (1994) *Europe and the Global Information Society: Recommendations to the European Council*, Brussels, 26 May.

Barnard, J., Broomhead, V., Godwin, L. and Smith, A. (1996) *Top Fifty European Media Owners*, London: Zenith Media, April.

Barnett, S. (2001) *Response to the DCMS on the Communications White Paper*, University of Westminster, February. Posted under 'Responses to the White Paper' at http://www.communicationswhitepaper.gov.uk/

BBC (2001) *BBC Response to White Paper, A New Future for Communications*, February.

BECTU (1994) *Review of Cross-Media Ownership*, submission to the DNH, London: BECTU.

Beltrame, F. (1996), 'Lawmaking in the European Union'. Paper prepared for the W G Hart Legal Workshop, Institute of Advanced Legal Studies.

Benoit, B. (2001) 'EMTV clear to approach suitors', *Financial Times*, 31 January: 30.

Betts, P. (2001) 'The medium is the message as Italian poll is glued to TV', *Financial Times*, 5 May: 6.

BMIG (British Media Industry Group) (1994) *The Future of the British Media Industry*, A Submission to the DNH, London, February.

BMIG (British Media Industry Group) (1995) *A New Approach to Cross-media Ownership*, submission to the DNH, London, February.

BSkyB (1996) *British Sky Broadcasting plc Annual Report 1996*.

Buckley, N. and Iskander, S. (2000) 'Vivendi, Seagram deal faces EU delay', *Financial Times*, 10 August: 22.

Carley, M. (1983) *Rational Techniques in Policy Analysis*, London: Policy Studies Institute Heinemann.

Cave, M. (1989) 'An Introduction to television economics', in G. Hughes and D. Vine (eds), *Deregulation and the Future of Commercial Television*, Aberdeen: Aberdeen University Press.

CE (1996) Secretariat memorandum prepared by the Directorate of Human Rights, 'Comparative table of national legislation of relevance in the area of media concentrations', (MM-CM (96) 4 Rev), Strasbourg, 25 July.

CE (1997a) Secretariat memorandum prepared by the Directorate of Human Rights, 'Report on media concentrations and pluralism in Europe (revised version)', MM-CM (97) 6, Strasbourg, 20 January.

CE (1997b) Secretariat memorandum prepared by the Directorate of Human Rights, 'Compilation of national reports on media concentrations (provisional version)', MM-CM (97) 10, Strasbourg, 21 July.

CEC, European Commission (1992) *Pluralism and Media Concentration in the Internal Market: An Assessment of the Need for Community Action*, COM(92) 480 final, Brussels, 23 December.

CEC (1994) *Communication to Parliament and Council: Follow-up to the Consultation Process Relating to the Green Paper on 'Pluralism and Media Concentration in the Internal Market – An Assessment of the Need for Community Action'* (COM [94] 353 final), 5 October.

CEC (1997) *Explanatory Memorandum* ('Media ownership in the Internal Market'), DG15, February.

Coase, R. (1937) 'The nature of the firm' reprinted in O. Williamson and S. Winter, *The Nature of the Firm: Origins, Evolution and Development*, Oxford: Oxford University Press, 1993. pp. 18–74.

Coleridge, N. (1993) *Paper Tigers*, London: Mandarin.

Collins, R. and Murroni, C. (1996) *New Media, New Policies: Media and Communications Strategies for the Future*, Cambridge: Polity Press.

Competition Commission (CC) (2000) *Carlton Communications Plc and Granada Group Plc and United News and Media plc: A Report on the Three Proposed Mergers*, Cm. 4781, London: HMSO.

Cowie, C. (1997) 'Competition problems in the transition to digital television', *Media Culture & Society*, 19: 679–85.

CPBF (2001) *The Response of CPBF to the White Paper*, London: Campaign for Press and Broadcasting Freedom, February.

Curran, J. and Seaton, J. (1997) *Power without Responsibility*, 5th edn, London: Routledge.

De Bens, E. and Ostbye, H. (1998) 'The European newspaper market', in D. McQuail and K. Siune (eds), *Media Policy: Convergence, Concentration and Commerce*, Euromedia Research Group, London: Sage. pp. 7–22.

Demers, D. (1999) *Global Media: Menace or Messiah?* NJ: Hampton Press.

Dinan, W. (2001) *The Republic of Ireland's Media Space: Ownership, Regulation and Policy*, Stirling Media Research Institute Report, Stirling, February.

DNH (Department of National Heritage) (1995a) *Media Ownership: The Government's Proposals*, Cm 2872, London: HMSO, May.

DNH (1995b) *Digital Terrestrial Broadcasting: The Goverment's proposals*, Cm 2946, London: HMSO, August.

DNH (1995c) 'Virginia Bottomley "liberates British broadcasters to be world leaders in the 21st century"', press release (DNH 252/95), 15 December.

Doyle, G. (1997) 'From "pluralism" to "media ownership": Europe's emergent policy on media concentrations navigates the doldrums', *Journal of*

*Information Law and Technology*, http://elj.strath.ac.uk/jilt/commsreg/ 97_3doyl/, October.

Doyle, G. (1998a) Consultant study on *Media Consolidation in Europe: The Impact on Pluralism*, Council of Europe, Committee of Experts on Media Concentrations and Pluralism (MM-CM), MM-CM (97) 12 rev, Strasbourg, January.

Doyle, G. (1998b) 'Towards a pan-European Directive? From "concentrations and pluralism" to "media ownership"', *Journal of Communications Law*, 3 (1): 11–15.

Doyle, G. (1998c), 'Regulation of media ownership and pluralism in Europe: can the European Union take us forward?', *Cardozo Arts & Entertainment Law Journal*, 16 (2–3): 451–73.

Doyle, G. (1999) 'Convergence: "a unique opportunity to evolve in previously unthought-of ways" or a hoax?' in C. Marsden and S. Verhulst (eds), *Convergence in European Digital TV Regulation*. London: Blackstone.

Doyle, G. (2000) 'The economics of monomedia and cross-media expansion: a study of the case favouring deregulation of TV and newspaper ownership', *Journal of Cultural Economics*, 24: 1–26.

DTI/DCMS (Department of Trade and Industry/ Department of Culture, Media and Sport) (1998) *Regulating Communications: Approaching Convergence in the Information Age*, Cm 4022, HMSO, July.

DTI/DCMS (2000) *A New Future for Communications*, Cm 5010, HMSO, December.

Editoriale L'Espresso (1993) 'Commentaire au livre vert de la Commission "Pluralisme et concentration des media dans le marché intérieur"', press release.

EIM (1997) *Expansion and Concentration of Media Companies in Europe*, Düsseldorf: European Institute of the Media.

(EP) European Parliament (1994) Report of the Committee on Culture, Youth, Education and the Media on the Commission Green Paper 'Pluralism and Media Concentration in the Internal Market', COM(92) 0480-C3-0035/93, Rapporteurs Mr Ben Fayot and Mr Dieter Schinzel, A3-0435, 5 January.

European Publishers Council (EPC) (1994) 'European Parliament resolution threatens Europe's position on the Information Superhighway', news release, January.

European Audiovisual Observatory (1997) *Statistical Yearbook*. Strasbourg: European Audiovisual Observatory.

European Federation of Magazine Publishers (FAEP) (1993) *Submission in Response to the Commission's Green Paper on Pluralism and Media Concentration in the Internal market*, April.

Feintuck, M. (1999) *Media Regulation, Public Interest and the Law*, Edinburgh: Edinburgh University Press.

Financial Times (Lex comment) (1995a) 'UK television', *Financial Times*, 16 December: 18.

Financial Times (Market report) (1995b) 'Bright TV picture', *Financial Times*, 16 December: 13.

Financial Times (Editorial comment) (2000) 'Tabloid power', *Financial Times* 1 November: 24.

Financial Times (Editorial comment) (2001) 'Internet profits', *Financial Times*, 15 January: 22.

Gabara, I. (1997) 'The EU should leave media rules to member states', *Wall Street Journal*, 25 March: 7.

GAH (1994) *Feasibility of Using Audience Measures to Assess Pluralism*, Position Paper, November, Strasbourg: DG XV.

Garnham, N. and Porter, V. (1994) *Evidence to the Review of Cross-Media Ownership*, Centre for Communication and Information Studies (CCIS), University of Westminster.

George, K., Joll, C. and Lynk, E. (1992) *Industrial Organisation*, 4th edn, London: Routledge.

Gibbons, T. (1998) *Regulating the Media*, 2nd edn, London: Sweet and Maxwell.

Goldberg, D., Prosser, T. and Verhulst, S. (1998) *Regulating the Changing Media: A Comparative Study*, Oxford: Clarendon Press.

Gomery, D. (1993) 'Who owns the media?' in A. Alexander, J. Owers and R. Carveth, *Media Economics: theory and practice*, Mahway, NJ: Lawrence Erlbaum Associates, pp. 47–70.

Graham, A. and Davies, G. (1997) *Broadcasting, Society and Policy in the Multimedia Age*, Luton: John Libbey Media.

Graham, D. (2001) *Responses to the Communications White Paper: Executive Summary*, David Graham & Associates, March. Posted under 'Responses to the White Paper' at http://www.communicationswhitepaper.gov.uk/

Granada (2001) *Granada Plc Response to the DTI/DCMS Communications White Paper*, February. Posted under 'Responses to the White Paper' at http://www.communicationswhitepaper.gov.uk/

Griffiths, A. and Wall, S. (1999) *Applied Economics*, 8th edn, Harlow: Prentice-Hall.

Harcourt, A. (1996) 'Regulating for media concentration: the emerging policy of the European Union', *Utilities Law Review*, 7(5) October: 202–10.

Harding, J. (2000a) 'Pearson and Li group to announce alliance in Asia', *Financial Times*, 3 July: 25.

Harding, J. (2000b) 'An overhaul? Yes, but [.]' (Creative Industries supplement pp. 2–3), *Financial Times*, 12 December.

Hargreaves, D. (2000a) 'New media, new rules', *Financial Times*, 7 July: 21.

Hargreaves, D. (2000b) 'Brussels to rule on media deals', *Financial Times*, 26 September: 36.

Hargreaves, D., Waters, R. and Harding, J. (2000a) 'Regulating the unknown', *Financial Times*, 7 September: 22.

Hargreaves, D., Owen, D. and Harding, J. (2000b) 'Vivendi merger plan cleared by EC', *Financial Times*, 14 October: 23.

Hargreaves, I. (2000) 'Dealing with cross media' (Creative Industries supplement p. 5), *Financial Times*, 5 December.

Hargreaves, I. (2001) 'Why is The Sun hot for Tony?' (Creative Industries supplement p. 5), *Financial Times*, 20 March.

Hirsch, M. and Petersen, V. (1998), 'European policy initiatives', in McQuail D and Siune K (eds) *Media Policy: Convergence, Concentration and Commerce*, Euromedia Research Group, London: Sage, pp. 207–24.

Hitchens, L. (1994) 'Media ownership and control: a European approach', *Modern Law Review*, 57(4) July: 585–601.

Hitchens, L. (1995) '"Get ready, fire, take aim": the regulation of cross-media ownership – an exercise in policy-making', *Public Law*, Winter: 620–41.

Hogwood, B. and Gunn, L. (1984) *Policy Analysis for the Real World*, Oxford: Oxford University Press.

Horsman, M. (2000) 'A swaggering predator called Granada' (Media Guardian, p. 3), *Guardian*, 17 July.

Hughes, J. (2000) 'The global marketplace: making sense of the future', in J. Hughes et al., *e-britannia: the communications revolution*, Luton: University of Luton Press. pp. 23–67.

Humphreys, P. (1996) *Mass Media and Media Policy in Westernn Europe*, (European Policy Research Unit Series) Manchester: Manchester University Press.

Humphreys, P. (1997) 'Power and control in the new media', Paper presented at the ECPR Workshop New Media and Political Communication, University of Manchester. 27 February.

Iosifides, P. (1996) 'Merger control and media pluralism in the European Union', *Communications Law*, 1(6): 247–9.

Independent Television Commission (ITC) (1994) *Memorandum on Media Ownership* (Submission to the DNH), London, 25 February.

ITC (1995) *Media Ownership: ITC Response to the Government's Proposals*, London, 29 August.

ITC (2000) 'ITC publishes views on the proposed acquisitions by Granada Group plc of UN&M plc or Carlton Communications plc', London: ITC press release 39/00, 12 May.

ITVA (ITV Association) (1997) 'ITV concerned about proposed EU Media Ownership Directive', press release, ITV Association, London, 17 March.

Kaitatzi-Whitlock, S. (1996) 'Pluralism and media concentration in Europe: media policy as industrial policy', *European Journal of Communication*, 11(4): 453–83.

Kapner, F. (2001) 'Telecom Italia to fight for TV deal', *Financial Times*, 19 January: 28.

Kleinwächter, W. (1998) 'Germany', in D. Goldberg, T. Prosser, and S. Verlulst (eds), *Regulating the Changing Media*, Oxford: Clarendon Press. pp. 29–60.

Lange, A. and Van Loon, A. (1991) *Pluralism, Concentration and Competition in the Media Sector*. Montpellier, Amsterdam: Institute of Audiovisual Telecommunications in Europe (IDATE) and Institute for Information Law (IVIR), December.

Larsen, P. and O'Connor, A. (2000a) 'Granada reaches for remote control in TV merger', *Financial Times*, 8 January: 16.

Larsen, P. and O'Connor, A. (2000b) 'Granada given an ace in ITV's game of cards', *Financial Times*, 15 July: 16.

Levin, P. (1997) *Making Social Policy: The Mechanisms of Government and Politics, and How To Investigate Them*, Buckingham: Open University Press.

Lipsey, R. and Chrystal, A. (1995) *Positive Economics*, 8th edn, Oxford: Oxford University Press.

Litman, B. (1998) 'The economics of television networks: new dimensions and new alliances' in A. Alexander, J. Owers and R. Carveth, *Media Economics: Theory and Practice*, 2nd edn, Mahway, NJ: Lawrence Erlbaum Associates. pp. 131–50.

MacLeod, V. (ed.) (1996) *Media Ownership and Control in the Age of Convergence*, London: International Institute of Communications.

Martin, S. (1993) *Industrial Economics: Economic Analysis and Public Policy*, 2nd edn, Englewood Cliffs: Prentice-Hall.

McEvoy, J. (1997) 'EU angers publishers by pushing on with media law', Reuters press release, 11 March.

Meier, W. and Trappel, J. (1998) 'Media concentration and the public interest', in D. McQuail and K. Siune (eds), *Media Policy: Convergence, Concentration and Commerce*, Euromedia Research Group, London: Sage. pp. 38–59.

MM-CM (1997) Secretariat memorandum prepared by the Directorate of Human Rights, *Report on Media Concentrations and Pluralism in Europe* (revised version), Council of Europe, MM-CM (97) 6, Strasbourg, 20 January.

Mortensen, F. (1993) *Study by a Consultant on the Notion of Access to the Market*, Council of Europe, Committee of Experts on Media Concentrations and Pluralism (MM-CM), MM-CM (93) 21, Strasbourg.

Moschandreas, M. (1994) *Business Economics*, London: Routledge.

Mounier, P. (1997) 'The concentration game', *The Bulletin*, EIM, Spring.

Mounier, P. and Robillard, S. (1994) *La Transparence dans le contrôle des médias*, Düsseldorf: EIM, November.

Murdock, G. and Golding, P. (1977) 'Capitalism, communication and class relations', in J. Curran, M. Gurevitch and J. Woollacott (eds), *Mass Communication and Society*, London: Edward Arnold. pp. 12–43.

Negrine, R. (1994) *Politics and the Mass Media in Britain*, 2nd edn, London: Routledge.

Newspaper Society (2001) *Submission to the Culture, Media and Sport Select Committee and to the DTI and DCMS*, February. Posted under 'Responses to the White Paper' at http://www.communicationswhitepaper.gov.uk/

NI (2001) *Response to the White Paper, A New Future for Communications*, February. Posted under 'Responses to the White Paper' at http://www.communicationswhitepaper.gov.uk/

NUJ (1994) *Cross-Media Ownership: A Submission to the National Heritage Ministry by the National Union of Journalists*, London: NUJ, February.

O'Connor, A. (2000) 'Blueprint for a 10-year regime' (Creative Industries supplement p. 3), *Financial Times*, 12 December.

Oliver, M. (2000) 'e-brittanica', in J. Hughes et al., *e-brittania: the communications revolution*, Luton: University of Luton Press. pp. 55–68.

Owen, B. and Wildman, S. (1992) *Video Economics*, Cambridge, MA: Harvard University Press.

Parsons, W. (1995) *Public Policy: An Introduction to the Theory and Practice of Policy Analysis*, Aldershot: Edward Elgar.

Peacock, A. (Chairman) (1986) *Report of the Committee on Financing the BBC*. Cm 9824, London: HMSO.

Pearson plc (1993) *Submission on the Commission's Green Paper: Pluralism and Media Concentration in the Internal Market*, London: Pearson.

Pearson plc (1994) *Submission to the DNH on Cross-Media Ownership Rules*, London: Pearson.

Picard, R. (Ed.) (2000) *Measuring Media Content, Quality and Diversity*, Turku, Finland: Turku School of Economics and Business Administration.

Prosser, T., Goldberg, D. and Verhulst, S. (1996) *The Impact of New Communications Technologies on Media Concentrations and Pluralism*, A report on behalf of MM-CM, University of Glasgow.

Roberts, D. and Brown, J. (2001) 'Soros and O'Reilly team up in telecom bid', *Financial Times*, 23 April: 1.

Robertson, G. and Nicol, A. (1992) *Media Law*, Harmondsworth: Penguin.

Sánchez-Tabernero, A. (1993) *La Concentration des médias en Europe*, Düsseldorf: EIM.

Scherer, F. and Ross, D. (1990) *Industrial Market Structure and Economic Performance*, 3rd edn, Boston: Houghton Mifflin.

Schlesinger, P. (1994) *The Scott Trust*, 2nd edn, London: The Scott Trust.

Schlesinger, P. and Doyle, G. (1995) 'Contradictions of economy and culture: the European Union and the information society', *Journal of European Cultural Policy*, 2 (1): 25–42.

Schumpeter, J. (1942) *Capitalism, Socialism and Democracy*, New York: Harper.

Seymour-Ure, C. K. (1991) *The British Press and Broadcasting since 1945*, Oxford: Blackwell.

Shepherd, W. (1979) *The Economics of Industrial Organisation*, Englewood Cliffs, NJ: Prentice-Hall.

Shew, W. and Stelzer, I. (1996) 'A policy framework for the media industries', in M. Beesley (ed.), *Markets and the Media: Competition, Regulation and the Interests of Consumers*, Institute of Economic Affairs, Readings 43. pp. 109–46.

Shooshan, H. and Cave, M. (2000) 'Media and telecoms regulation in converging markets', in Hughes, J. et al. *e-brittania: the communications revolution*, Luton: University of Luton Press. pp. 71–84.

SMG (2001) *A Submission from SMG plc in Response to 'A New Future for Communications'*, February. Posted under 'Responses to the White Paper' at http://www.communicationswhitepaper.gov.uk/

Smith, A. (1937) *An Inquiry into the Nature and Causes of the Wealth of Nations*, New York: Modern Library edn.

Smith, B. (1976) *Policy Making in British Government: An Analysis of Power and Rationality*, Oxford: Martin Robertson.

Snoddy, R. (1995a) 'News groups urge easing of ownership rules', *Financial Times*, 1 March:

Snoddy, R. (1995b) 'Music to the media lobbyists' ears', *Financial Times*, 25 May:

Snoddy, R. (1995c) 'ITV bidding war likely after government rethink', *Financial Times*, 16 December: 18.

Styles, P. et al. (1996) *Public Policy Issues Arising from Telecommunications and Audiovisual Convergence*, A Report for the European Commission, KPMG, September.

Trinity Mirror (2001) *Response to the White Paper*, February. Posted under 'Responses to the White Paper' at http://www.communicationswhitepaper.gov.uk/

Tucker, E. (1997) 'EU media initiative bogged down', *Financial Times*, 13 March: 23.

Tunstall, J. and Palmer, M. (1991) *Media Moguls*, London: Routledge.

Weatherill, S. and Beaumont, P. (1995) *EC Law: The Essential Guide to the Legal Workings of the European Community*, 2nd edn, Harmondsworth: Penguin.

Williams, G. (1994) *Evidence to Cross Media Ownership Review Submitted by the Campaign for Press and Broadcasting Freedom*, London: CPBF.

Williamson, O. (1975) *Markets and Hierarchies: Analysis and Antitrust Implications*, New York: Free Press.

Williamson, O. and Winter, S. (eds) (1993) *The Nature of the Firm: Origins, Evolution and Development*, Oxford: Oxford University Press.

Wirth, M. and Bloch, H. (1995) 'Industrial organization theory and media industry analysis', *Journal of Media Economics*, 8 (2) :15–26.

Zerdick, A. (1993) 'Zwischen Frequenzen und Paragraphen: die Landesmedienanstalten als institutionalisierter Kompromiss', *Bertelsmann Briefe*, 129: 60–2.

# Index